BRITISH
LOC
1989

C000262810

LONDON

IAN ALLAN LTD

INTRODUCTION

The serious railway enthusiast will realise that 1988 saw further major changes to BR's traction. Locomotives are extremely costly and where a multiple-unit can be introduced, as is the case with all Network SouthEast and Provincial Sector services, this is being implemented as quickly as practicable. InterCity is concentrating its future on electric locomotives operating push-pull trains on the East Coast and West Coast main lines. The tighter control of resources permitted by Sector management has led to an overall reduction in the locomotive fleet.

A brief analysis of 1988 and the programme for 1989 indicates that Class 03 will be reduced to one operating on the mainland, but two will continue to operate on the Isle of Wight. The Parcels Sector will require fewer shunters as the maintenance of its van fleet is concentrated on two depots. No major overhauls are being carried out on Class 20 locomotives and they will gradually be displaced, but they will make history early in 1989 when up to eight will enter private ownership with Hunslet-Barclay for hire to the operators of special purpose trains such as weedkillers. Another side effect of the stricter adherance of locomotive operation to the financing Sector's duties has been the reduction of the maximum operating speed of many in the Freight and Departmental fleets. This also reduces the frequency of routine maintenance and helps reduce the quantity of spares required. Many Class 31/1s are due to become surplus over the next year. Refurbishment of the Class 37 fleet will cease with the entry to traffic of the last Class 37/7 conversion in February 1989. Further Class 47s will also gradually become surplus. The last Class 40 has been replaced as the celebrity Charter Sub-Sector locomotive by the final Class 45/1. Overhauls have also ceased on Class 50, and by October many should be replaced by the Class 47/7 fleet displaced from Scotland by new Class 158 DMUs. Railfreight runs a substantial number of petroleum, construction (stone and aggregates) and steel trains that require the uneconomic double-heading of heavy trains. It is therefore due to take delivery of the first of 100 Class 60 locomotives in June, thus gradually eliminating, from 1990, over 200 of the current fleet.

Commencing in May 1989 the first 10 Class 91 locomotives will be available to haul King's Cross-Leeds services. This will release some Class 43 IC125 power cars for mid-life re-engining whilst InterCity determines the long-term future of those displaced by the East Coast main line electrification. There are no plans to displace those on InterCity Midland, Western or Cross-Country services. The gradual introduction of Class 90 locomotives and push-pull operation of West Coast main line services will also allow the withdrawal of Classes 81, 83 and most of Class 85. An accident at Newcastle caused two IC125 coaches to be withdrawn. Although new Mk 4 coaches are to be introduced on the East Coast route, other IC125 routes require additional or strengthened rakes to cater for traffic growth, but no significant cascading is envisaged until May 1990.

Roger Wood, January 1989

Important Note

A significant number of changes, particularly relating to Sector allocation codes, were announced by BR after this book went to press. Where possible these have been incorporated. A complete summary by sub-Sector and a 'Late News' amendment list corrected to February 1989 appear later in this book. Our modern scene magazine *Motive Power Monthly*, produces a fully detailed and up-to-date guide to changes as advised by BR.

Equipment and Special Characteristics

This year's format has been further revised as part of our policy of continued improvement and clarity for users. Equipment that is standard to a locomotive class is shown in the heading and special characteristics (variations) are indicated by a symbol against the individual locomotive number. An innovation this year is the inclusion of the official BRB DMEE locomotive diagram code which is made up of locomotive class, sub-class, an alphabetical variation code, and a train brake type code (A=air, V=vacuum or X=dual air and vacuum). The variations can apply to weight, train heating, maximum speed and major components fitted and are indicated in the class headings. Characteristic codes used comply where possible with those used officially by BR.

Locomotives:

B	Cab-to-shore radio communication (BR telephone network)
C	Refurbished cab (Classes 08 and 09)
H	Drawbar tested for emergency haulage of IC125 trains (to be advised)
K*	Snowplough brackets for fitting three-part miniature snowploughs
L	Fixed beam headlight/spotlight
M	Driver-only operation equipment
N*	Remote control radio (experimental)
P	Push-pull operation by Time Division Multiplex system
R	Radio Electronic Token Block
S	Slow Speed Control
T	Transponder code transmitter (locomotive number to shore)
U	Electric train heating equipment non-operational
X	Additional fuel capacity (see class heading for tank capacity)
Z*	Remote control (for MGR trains at equipped power stations; out of use experiment)

60, 75 or 80mph maximum operating speed, long-term restrictions

InterCity 125 Coaches:

P	Public payphone
R	Refurbished interiors

Locomotive Liveries

BR has announced its intention to standardise liveries to five main variations, although standard blue still predominates at this time. Colour photographs in this booklet generally indicate the following styles. Minor variations to styles are not indicated here but special liveries are indicated in class headings.

I   **InterCity.** Classes 43, 86, 87, 89, 90 and 91 are authorised to carry the branding 'INTERCITY' and swallow emblem. Other InterCity Sector locomotives carry the livery without the branding and emblem. The number is to be placed on the cabside, near the bottom, by the driving position. Parcels Sector diesel locomotives of Classes 31/4 and 47/4, and electric locomotives, are intended to carry this unbranded livery with the number below the cab window.

Is   **InterCity.** Old style with red waistband and ScotRail lettering.
Ps **Provincial.** Old style InterCity with blue waistband and ScotRail lettering.
PT **Provincial.** Trans-Pennine two-tone blue.
F   **Railfreight.** Old grey livery, later examples with red band round sole-bar.
F   **Railfreight.** New two-tone grey livery, without sub-Sector symbols.
FA **Railfreight Construction.** Blue and yellow rectangles.
FE **Railfreight Coal.** Black diamonds on yellow background.
FG **Railfreight Distribution.** Red diamonds on yellow background.
FM **Railfreight Metals & Automotive.** Blue and yellow chevrons.
FP **Railfreight Petroleum.** Blue ripple lines on yellow background.
FX **Railfreight General.** Red and yellow rectangles.
N   **Network SouthEast.** Classes 47 and 50 only.
D   **Departmental.** Falcon grey livery.
★   **Special livery.** See class heading.

Coupling of Locomotives

Main line diesel locomotives can be operated in multiple (driven only from leading locomotive) with locomotives fitted with compatible control equipment. Classes 20, 31, 33 and 37 have electro-pneumatic control and carry a 'blue star' symbol above each buffer. Class 50 locomotives carry an 'orange square' symbol and can only multiple with others of this class, whilst Classes 56 and 58 are in the 'red diamond' code group. Other classes, and these when not electronically compatibly coupled, are able to operate in tandem — a separate driver controlling each locomotive. Multiple-working restrictions applicable to electronic locomotives are indicated in the appropriate class headings. When operating in multiple or tandem, restrictions applicable to one locomotive (maximum speed etc) must be adhered to by the assisting locomotive(s).

Level of Repair and Maintenance Facility

In April 1987 BR introduced a new maintenance policy for all traction and coaching stock. Under the scheme, depots and workshops are classified on a scale of 1 to 6, called Levels, determined by the facilities available and work effected at each location.

The larger establishments, Level 5, normally have separate workshops to carry out this category of repair and are not necessarily answerable to the Sector which 'owns' the main depot.

Definition

Level	Facility	Description
1	Fuel point	Facility for dispensing fuel, oil and water to diesel locomotives and/or DMUs. Minor servicing to EMUs. Manned by unskilled staff.
2	Servicing	Capable of undertaking 'A' exam work and occasional 'B' exams and multiple-units together with work arising and brake blocking also full maintenance for diesel shunter locomotives. For coaching stock some cleaning, chemical emission toilet disposal, environmental checks, two daily exams, weekly exams and brake blocking. The facility will have a covered pit, a small store and be manned by skilled staff.
3	Maintenance	This facility will have a Traction and Rolling Stock allocation and be capable of carrying out all levels of exams and the majority of repairs arising. It will have covered pits, staff accomodation, light lifting and jacking facilities. A full range of equipment will be available to meet all exam requirements. Multiple-units and coaching stock all levels of exams, code 'C' cleaning, patch painting and some body repair.
4	Maintenance and repair	As for level 3 but having an additional capability for heavier repairs. The depot will be well equipped with cranes and/or heavy lifting jacks for bogie removal and possibly a wheel lathe.
5	Heavy repair	A facility capable of undertaking unplanned heavy repairs and collision damage arising at lower-level facilities. May also have the facility for lower level of classified repair, limited component refurbishment and half life component exchange. Fuelling facilities are not necessarily provided.
6	Workshop	A main workshop with full facilities for undertaking all levels of classified and unclassified repairs.

	Level			Main Sector(s)	Full Maintenance
	Loco	HST		(Locomotives)	Classes Allocated
AB	2	2	Aberdeen HS	P/I	08/0
AF	2		Ashford, Chart Leacon T&RSMD	N	08/0, 09
AN	2		Allerton SD	F	08/0
AY	2		Ayr TMD	F	08/0
BD	1		Birkenhead North EMUD	P	03, 97/7
BI	2		Brighton T&RSMD	N	—
BL	2		Blyth (Cambois) SD	F	—
BM	2		Bournemouth West EMUD	N	—
BN	2	4	Bounds Green T&RSMD	I/R	—
BR	4	5	Bristol Bath Road TMD	I/R	08/0, 47/4
BS	3		Bescot TMD	D	08/0, 31/1, 31/4
BW	1		Barrow	F	—
BX	2		Buxton TMD	F	—
BY	2		Bletchley TMD	N	08/0
BZ	2		St Blazey SD	F	—
CA	2		Cambridge (Coldhams Lane) TMD	R	08/0
CD	4		Crewe TMD	I/F	08/0, 31/1, 31/4, 47/0, 47/3, 47/4, 97/2, 97/4
CE	4		Crewe ETD	F	85
CF	4		Cardiff Canton TMD	F	08/0, 09, 37/0, 37/5, 37/7, 37/9, 47/0, 47/3, 47/9, 56, 97/8
CH	1		Chester TMD	P	—
CL	2		Carlisle Upperby	P	08/0
CR	2		Colchester SD	F	—
DL	5		Doncaster Major Depot, BRML	D	08
DR	2		Doncaster TMD	F	08/0
DY	2	4	Derby, Etches Park T&RSMD	I	08/0
EC		4	Edinburgh, Craigentinny T&RSMD	I	43
ED	4		Eastfield, Glasgow TMD	I/P/F	08/0, 20, 26/0, 26/1, 37/0, 37/4, 47/0, 47/4, 47/7
EH	4		Eastleigh T&RSMD	D/F/N/R	08/0, 09, 33/0, 33/1
EX	2		Exeter St Davids SD	F/N	—
FH	2		Frodingham T&RSMD	F	—

	Level				Main Sector(s) (Locomotives)	Full Maintenance Classes Allocated
	Loco	HST				
FW	1			Fort William	P/F	—
GD	2			Gateshead TMD	F	08/0
GL	2			Gloucester SD	F	08/0
GM	2			Grangemouth SD	F	—
GW	4			Glasgow, Shields EMD	I	81
HA	2			Haymarket TMD	F	08/0
HD	1			Holyhead SD	F	—
HO	2			Holbeck SD	F	08/0
HT		4		Heaton T&RSMD	I/P	43
IL	2			Ilford EMD	I/N	—
IM	4			Immingham TMD	F	08/0, 20, 37/0, 37/3, 47/0, 47/3, 47/4
IP	1			Ipswich HS	F	—
IS	4			Inverness TMD	P	08/0, 37/0, 37/4, 47/4
KY	2			Knottingley SD	F	—
	1			Kings Lynn	F	—
LA	5	4		Laira TMD	I/N	08/0, 37/4, 37/5, 43, 50, 50/1
LE	2	2		Landore TMD	F	08/0, 08/9
LG	2			Longsight EMD	I	—
LO	2			Longsight TMD	R	08/0
LR	2			Leicester SD	F	—
MG	2			Margam FP	F	—
ML	3			Motherwell TMD	F	08/0, 20, 37/0, 37/3
MR	2			March SD	D	—
NC	2			Norwich, Crown Point T&RSMD	P	08/0
NH	1			Newton Heath TMD	P	—
NL	4	5		Neville Hill T&RSMD	I	08/0, 43
OC/OO	4	4		Old Oak Common T&RSMDs	N/I	08/0, 43, 47/4, 50
PB	2			Peterborough SD	F	—

	Level				Main Sector(s)	Full Maintenance
	Loco	HST			(Locomotives)	Classes Allocated
PH	1			Perth LIP	R	08/0
PM		4		St Phillips Marsh HSTD	I	43
PZ	1	2		Penzance SD	I	—
RG	2			Reading TMD	R	08/0
RL	2			Ripple Lane SD	F	—
RY	1			Ryde, Isle of Wight EMD	D	03, 97/8
SB	2			Shirebrook SD	F	—
SF	4			Stratford TMD	F	08/0, 31/1, 37/0, 37/3, 37/7, 47/0, 47/3, 47/4
SG				Slade Green T&RSMD	D	97/8
SL	4			Stewarts Lane T&RSMD	I/F	33/0, 33/2, 73/0, 73/1
SP	2			Springs Branch, Wigan TMD	F	08/0
SR	5			Stratford Major Depot		—
SU	2			Selhurst T&RSMD	N	08/0, 09
SY	1			Saltley LIP	F	—
TE	4			Thornaby TMD	F	08/0, 20, 31/1, 37/0, 37/5, 47/0, 47/3, 47/4
TI	4			Tinsley TMD	F	08/0, 31/1, 31/4, 37/0, 37/3, 37/5, 47/0, 47/3
TJ	2			Thornton SD	F	—
TO	4			Toton TMD	F	08/0, 20, 56, 58
TS	2			Tyseley TMD	R	—
WN	4			Willesden TMD	I	86/1, 86/2, 86/4, 86/5, 87/0, 87/1
WY	2			Westbury Loco SD	F	—
YK	2			York LIP (Wagon Works)	F	08/0
ZG	6			Eastleigh BRML	D	08/0
ZH	5			Springburn BRML	D	08/0
ZN		5		Wolverton BRML	D	08/0

	Level			Main Sector(s)	Full Maintenance
	Loco	HST		(Locomotives)	Classes Allocated
BREL Works					
ZC	6		Crewe	C	08/0
ZD		6	Derby Carriage	C	—
ZE	6	6	Derby Locomotive	C	08/0
ZR			York Carriage	C	—

Private Works

ZB	5		RFS Engineering Doncaster	C	08/0

British Railways Board

ZQ   BRB Headquarters
     (Traction on acceptance and Private Owner stock)

Sectors:
C: Private owner
D: Departmental (HQ)
F: Railfreight
I: InterCity
N: Network SouthEast
P: Provincial
R: Parcels

CLASS 03   SHUNTER   0-6-0

Built: British Rail 1959-62.
Engine: Gardner 8L3 8cyl, 4-stroke, 204hp (152kW).
Weight: 31 tonnes.
Brake force: 13 tonnes.
Maximum tractive effort: 15,300lb (68.1kN).
Power/control equipment: Mechanical. Wilson-Drewry type CA5 R7 five-speed epicyclic gearbox; Vulcan-Sinclair type 23 fluid coupling.

Dimensions: *Diagram* 03-OBX 26ft L × 8.5ft W × 12.2ft H. *Diagram* 03-ODX 26ft L × 8.5ft W × 11.8ft H
Route availability: 1.
Fuel: 300gal.
Maximum operating speed: 28.5mph.
Train brakes: Dual Air and Vacuum.
Standard equipment: Sanding gear.

Sectors:
Network SouthEast: **NXXA:** General
Provincial: **PXXA:** General.
Railfreight: **FGZZ:** Distribution (Speedlink). **FTZZ:** Chemicals.
Special livery: *Green:* 03162.
Note: 03162 carries pre-TOPS number D2162.

Loc No	Dia	SC	Liv	Pool	Dep
03073	BX			PXXA	BD
03162	BX		★	FTZZ	BD
Birkenhead South 1879-1985					
03170	BX			FGZZ	BD
03179	DX			NXXA	RY

CLASS 08/0   SHUNTER   0-6-0

Built: British Rail 1953-62.
Engine: English Electric 6cyl, 6KT of 400hp (315kW).
Weight: 49 tonnes.
Dimensions: 29.3ft L × 8.5ft W × 12.7ft H.
Brake force: 19 tonnes.
Maximum tractive effort: 35,000lb (156kN).
Power/control equipment: Two English Electric EE 506 traction motors; double reduction gear drive; main generator EE 801.
Route availability: 5.
Fuel: 668gal.

Diagram	Train Brake	Max Speed	Voltage
08-0AV	Vacuum	20mph	90
08-0BX	Dual	20mph	110
08-0CA	Air	20mph	90
08-0DV	Vacuum	15mph	90
08-0EX	Dual	15mph	90
08-0FA	Air	15mph	90
08-0KX	Dual	15mph	110

Standard equipment: Sanding gear.

Sectors:
Private owner: (unofficial codes): **CBRE:** BREL '88, **CRFS:** RFS Engineering.
Departmental: **DBMS:** BRML. **DCMB:** DCE Midland. **DCSB:** DCE Southern. **DRTC:** Research. **DWCS:** DMEE.
InterCity: **IANB:** Anglia. **ICCA:** Cross Country. **ICHA:** Charter. **IECA:** East Coast route. **IMLA:** Midland Lines. **IWCA:** West Coast route. **IWRA:** Western Region.
Network SouthEast: **NXXA:** General.
Parcels: **RXLA:** General.
Provincial: **PXXA:** General.
Railfreight: **FAZZ:** Construction. **FEZZ:** Coal (MGR). **FGZZ:** Distribution (Speedlink). **FHZZ:** Coal. **FMZZ:** Metals. **FPZZ:** Petroleum. **FTZZ:** Chemicals. **FVZZ:** Automotive. **FXXA:** General. **FXXL:** General. **LNRS:** Distribution (Freightliner).
Special liveies: *Black:* 08601, 08730, 08867, 08907.
Great Eastern blue: 08833.
Green: 08011, 08556, 08604, 08772/93, 08869, 08944.

Loc No	Dia	SC	Liv	Pool	Dep	Loc No	Dia	SC	Liv	Pool	Dep
08011	DV		★	DCWA	BY	08415	EX			LNRS	AN
Haversham						08416	FA			FQZZ	TO
						08417	FA			DWCS	SF
08182	DV			CBRE	ZR	08418	FA			FGZZ	DR
D3236						08419	FA			FGZZ	KD
						08421	FA			FHZZ	GD
08202	AV			FHZZ	CF	08428	FA			FHZZ	DY
08250	DV			FXXL	NC	08434	DV			FEZZ	TI
08258	DV			DWCS	CA	08436	DV			FEZZ	TI
08308	DV			RXLA	TI	08440	FA			DWCS	SF
08309	DV			RXLA	HO	08441	FA			FHZZ	GD
08335	DV			CRFS	ZB	08442	FA			FHZZ	GD
Terence						08445	FA	C		FGZZ	IM
						08447	FA			FGZZ	KD
08375	AV			FHZZ	CF	08448	FA			FGZZ	DY
08388	FA	C		FGZZ	IM	08449	FA			FTZZ	HO
08389	FA	C		FGZZ	NL	08451	EX	C		IWCA	WN
08390	FA			FHZZ	LE	08454	EX			FGZZ	WN
08393	FA	C		DWCS	SF	08460	FA			FGZZ	NC
08397	FA	C		FGZZ	IM	08463	FA			FTZZ	DY
08399	FA			FGZZ	DY	08466	FA	C	F	FGZZ	BS
08401	FA			FXXL	IM	08468	DV			PXXA	SP
08402	FA			FHZZ	AN	08470	DV			CBRE	ZC
08405	FA	C		FGZZ	IM	08472	FA			LNRS	CD
08407	FA			FGZZ	NC	08479	DV			FXXL	CF
08410	FA	E		FGZZ	BR	08480	FA			IWRA	OC
08411	FA			DWCS	TE	Old Oak Common 1882-1982					
08413	FA			LNRS	SF						
08414	CA			LNRS	SF						

Loc No	Dia	SC	Liv	Pool	Dep	Loc No	Dia	SC	Liv	Pool	Dep
08481	EX	c		FGZZ	CF	08536	KX			IMLA	DY
08482	FA			FPZZ	AN	08537	KX	c	F	FXXL	IM
08483	FA			IWRA	BR	08538	KX			RXLA	CA
08484	FA			DBMS	ZN	08539	KX			DWCS	CA
08485	FA			FMZZ	AN	08540	KX	c		DWCS	CA
08489	FA			FGZZ	GD	08541	KX			FXXL	SF
08492	FA	c		FGZZ	TI	08542	KX			FXXL	SF
08493	FA			FHZZ	CF	08543	KX			FHZZ	TI
08495	EX			FGZZ	CA		*Rotherwood*				
	Bury										
						08544	KX			FXXL	GD
08496	FA			FGZZ	CA	08556	AV		★	ICHA	OC
08498	FA			FGZZ	NC	08561	EX	c		DWCS	AY
08499	FA			FXXL	YK	08562	EX			RXLA	DR
08500	EX	c		FXXL	YK		*The Doncaster Postman*				
	Thomas 1										
						08565	EX			DWCS	ML
08506	FA			DWCS	TE	08567	EX			DWCS	YK
08507	FA	c		FGZZ	GD	08568	EX	c		ICCA	ML
08508	DV			FXXL	TI	08569	EX	c		FGZZ	AN
08509	FA			FHZZ	TI	08570	EX			FGZZ	HA
	Wath ETD 41F					08571	EX			ICCA	HA
						08573	EX			DCMB	WN
08510	FA	c		FGZZ	DR	08575	EX	c		FXXL	TE
08511	FA			FTZZ	DY	08576	EX			DWCS	LA
08512	FA			FHZZ	GD	08577	EX	K		FXXL	GD
08514	FA			FGZZ	DR	08578	EX			RXLA	GD
08515	FA			FHZZ	GD	08580	EX			FGZZ	CA
08516	FA			DWCS	HO	08581	EX	CK		FAZZ	ML
08517	FA			FGZZ	BS	08582	FA	c		FGZZ	TE
08519	FA	c		FGZZ	TE	08583	EX			FXXL	YK
08521	FA			FXXL	GD	08584	EX			DWCS	LA
08523	EX			FGZZ	OC	08585	EX			RXLA	CD
08525	KX	c		FXXL	YK	08586	FA			DWCS	AY
08526	KX			FGZZ	CA	08587	EX			DWCS	GD
08527	KX			RXLA	SF	08588	EX	c		FXXL	TE
08528	KX			DWCS	CA	08589	EX	c		FGZZ	CF
08529	KX			DWCS	CA	08590	EX	c		FGZZ	NL
08530	KX			DWCS	NC	08591	EX	K		FGZZ	AY
08531	KX			FXXL	SF	08593	EX			FXXL	SF
08532	KX			FAZZ	AN	08594	EX			FXXL	CA
08533	KX			FGZZ	SF		*Ely*				
08534	KX			RXLA	SP						
	Edge Hill					08595	EX			FXXL	YK
						08597	EX			RXLA	TO
08535	KX	c	F	FHZZ	BS	08599	EX	c		FGZZ	CD
	George										

Loc No	Dia	SC	Liv	Pool	Dep
08601	EX	C	★	FVZZ	BS
Spectre					
08603	EX			FMZZ	BS
08604	EX	C	★	FMZZ	BS
Phantom					
08605	EX	C		DWCS	YK
08607	EX	C		FGZZ	DR
08609	EX			IWCA	WN
08610	EX	C		FEZZ	BS
08611	EX			RXLA	LO
08612	EX			DCMB	WN
08613	EX			FHZZ	CD
08614	EX	C		RXLA	WN
08615	EX			FMZZ	AN
08616	EX	C		PXXA	BS
08617	EX			RXLA	WN
08618	EX			FXXL	GD
08619	EX			DCMB	LO
08620	EX			FGZZ	ML
08622	EX			RXLA	DY
08623	EX	C		FHZZ	TO
08624	EX			FXXL	LO
08625	EX			RXLA	WN
08627	FA			FGZZ	SF
08628	EX			DCMB	BY
08629	EX			DBMS	ZN
Wolverton					
08630	EX			FGZZ	ML
08631	EX	C	N	FGZZ	CA
Eagle					
08632	EX	C		RXLA	IM
08633	EX			RXLA	CD
08634	EX			RXLA	OC
08635	EX			IWCA	CD
08637	EX	C		FGZZ	CF
08638	EX			DWCS	CA
Cambridge					
08641	KX	E		ICCA	LA
08642	BX			DBMS	ZG
08643	KX	E		IWRA	BR
08644	KX	E	I	ICCA	LA
Ponsendane					

Loc No	Dia	SC	Liv	Pool	Dep
08645	KX	E		IWRA	LA
Friary					
08646	KX			FXXL	LE
08647	KX			DBMS	DL
08648	BX			IWCA	WN
08649	KX			FGZZ	OC
08650	BX			FXXL	EH
08651	KX	E		IWRA	OC
08652	KX	K		FXXL	CF
08653	BX			DWCS	SU
08654	KX	CK		FGZZ	CF
08655	BX			FXXL	SF
08656	FA			FGZZ	BY
08657	FA			DWCS	YK
08658	EX			IANB	NC
08659	FA			LNRS	HO
08660	DV			FHZZ	CF
08661	FA			FGZZ	NL
08662	EX	C		FXXL	YK
08663	FA	E		FTZZ	LA
08664	EX	C		FGZZ	CF
08665	EX	C		FXXL	IM
08666	EX			DCMB	LO
08667	EX			FGZZ	NL
08668	EX	C		FXXL	CF
08669	FA			LNRS	AN
08670	FA			LNRS	WN
08672	FA			FGZZ	BS
08673	EX		I	ICCA	LO
Piccadilly					
08675	EX	C		FGZZ	AY
08676	EX			RXLA	LO
08677	EX	C		IWCA	WN
08680	KX			IWCA	AB
Northern Lights					
08682	EX	C		DWCS	DR
08683	EX			IWCA	WN
08685	EX			FXXL	NC
08686	FA			FHZZ	AN
08688	FA			FVZZ	AN
08689	FA			DWCS	SF
08690	EX			FGZZ	KD
08691	EX			FHZZ	TI
Escafeld					

Loc No	Dia	SC	Liv	Pool	Dep	Loc No	Dia	SC	Liv	Pool	Dep
08692	EX	c		DWCS	BS	08741	KX	c		IECA	GD
08693	EX			FGZZ	AY	08742	KX			RXLA	CD
08694	EX			FMZZ	CD	08743	KX	c		RXLA	IM
08695	EX			FGZZ	CD	08744	KX			RXLA	SP
08696	FA			NXXA	WN	08745	KX			FXXL	IM
08697	EX			RXLA	TO	08746	KX			RXLA	CD
08698	FA			DWCS	SF	08747	KX			FXXL	GD
08699	EX			FGZZ	CD	08748	KX			RXLA	NC
08700	FA			FGZZ	BS	08749	KX			FXXL	TI
08701	EX			FXXL	HO		*Great Central*				
08702	EX			DCMB	CD						
08703	FA			FGZZ	AN	08750	KX	c		FGZZ	SF
08704	EX			RXLA	BY	08751	KX	c		FXXL	IM
08705	FA			FGZZ	CA	08752	KX			IANB	NC
08706	EX	c		FGZZ	HO	08753	KX			PXXA	IS
08707	FA			FHZZ	HO		*Kinnoul K.D*				
08708	FA			LNRS	NC						
08709	EX			FXXL	SF	08754	KX			FGZZ	IS
08710	EX			DWCS	HA	08755	KX	c		FGZZ	HA
08711	EX	c		FGZZ	CA	08756	KX			FXXL	LE
08712	EX			DWCS	PH	08757	KX	c		DWCS	CA
08713	FA			FGZZ	CA	08758	KX			FXXL	SF
08714	EX			FXXL	CA	08759	KX			FMZZ	BS
08715	DV			FXXL	SF	08760	BX			FXXL	EH
08716	DV			DWCS	CA	08761	KX			PXXA	HA
08717	EX			IWCA	IS	08762	KX			PXXA	PH
08718	EX			IWCA	HA	08763	KX			DWCS	HA
08719	EX			DWCS	YK	08765	KX		★	IWCA	BS
08720	FA	c	P	PXXA	HA	08766	KX			DWCS	NL
08721	EX		R	RXLA	LO	08767	KX			DWCS	NC
	Starlet					08768	KX	c		IWCA	KD
						08769	DV			FHZZ	LE
08723	EX			RXLA	DR	08770	FA			DWCS	TE
08724	EX	c		FGZZ	SF	08771	KX			FXXL	YK
08725	EX			FGZZ	ML	08772	EX		★	DWCS	NC
08727	EX			FHZZ	AY		*Camulodunum*				
08729	FA			FHZZ	DR						
08730	EX		★	RXLA	HA	08773	EX			FHZZ	HO
08731	EX			PXXA	ML	08775	EX			DWCS	NC
08732	EX	c		FGZZ	ML	08776	FA	c		FHZZ	HO
08733	EX	c		DWCS	ML	08777	EX			DWCS	YK
08734	EX	c		RXLA	IM	08778	EX			FGZZ	GL
08735	EX	c		FHZZ	AY	08779	EX			FGZZ	LE
08737	KX			FGZZ	CD	08780	EX	c		FGZZ	LE
08738	KX	c		FGZZ	ML	08781	EX			FGZZ	GL
08739	KX			FGZZ	CD	08782	FA			FHZZ	HO
08740	KX			FXXL	SF	08783	EX			FXXL	HO
						08784	EX			DCMB	CD

Loc No	Dia	SC	Liv	Pool	Dep	Loc No	Dia	SC	Liv	Pool	Dep
08785	FA	E		FHZZ	CF	08830	BX			NXXA	EH
08786	FA	C		FGZZ	TE	08831	BX			DCSB	EH
08787	EX			FXXL	CF	08832	KX	C	F	FGZZ	BS
08788	EX			FPZZ	DY	08833	BX	C	★	IECA	SF
	Caergybi						*Liverpool Street Pilot*				
08789	FA			DCMB	BY	08834	KX	C	FG	FGZZ	SF
08790	EX			PXXA	LO	08835	KX	E		FXXL	CF
08791	FA			FEZZ	HA	08836	KX			RXLA	CF
08792	FA	C		FGZZ	LA	08837	BX			DCSB	SU
08793	FA		★	DWCS	HA	08838	KX			DCMB	SP
08794	EX			FXXL	NL	08839	KX			DWCS	LA
08795	EX	C		FGZZ	GL	08840	KX			RXLA	LA
08796	FA			FHZZ	CF	08841	KX			IWCA	BS
08797	EX			DWCS	GD	08842	KX			RXLA	DY
08798	EX	C		DWCS	LE	08843	KX			DCMB	CD
08799	EX			FGZZ	GL		*Holyhead*				
08800	EX			FGZZ	BR						
08801	EX			FXXL	BZ	08844	KX	C		RXLA	CL
08802	EX	C		FGZZ	GD	08845	BX			NXXA	EH
08803	EX	C		FGZZ	RG	08846	KX			IWCA	AN
08804	EX	C		FXXL	OC	08847	BX			DCSB	EH
08805	EX	C	F	RXLA	BS	08848	KX			FXXL	CF
08806	FA		F	FXXL	HO	08849	KX			FGZZ	LA
08807	EX			RXLA	BY	08850	KX			FXXL	RG
08808	EX			IWCA	CL	08851	KX			PXXA	ML
08809	EX			FHZZ	AN	08853	KX	CR		FGZZ	ML
08810	FA			DWCS	NC	08854	BX			ICCA	SU
08811	CA			LNRS	WN	08855	KX			RXLA	AB
08813	EX	C		DWCS	DR		*Hatton Castle*				
08814	FA			DRTC	DY						
08815	EX			DCMB	SP	08856	KX			FGZZ	AN
08817	EX	C		FXXL	TE	08857	KX	C		RXLA	TI
	Thornaby						*Darnall*				
08818	EX	C		FHZZ	CF	08858	KX			IWCA	AN
08819	EX	C		FGZZ	BR	08859	KX			DWCS	NC
08820	FA			LNRS	LO	08865	EX			RXLA	CA
08821	EX			RXLA	OC	08866	EX			DWCS	DR
08822	EX			RXLA	CF	08867	EX	C	★	RXLA	TE
08823	EX			LNRS	CD		*Ralph Easby*				
08824	FA			FHZZ	DR						
08825	FA			FGZZ	WN	08868	EX			IANB	NC
08826	FA			FGZZ	CL	08869	EX		★	FXXL	NC
08827	FA			FGZZ	CL		*The Canary*				
08828	FA			DWCS	SF						
08829	FA			FQZZ	TO						

15

Loc No	Dia	SC	Liv	Pool	Dep
08870	EX			FHZZ	TI
	Millhouses 41C				
08871	EX			FXXL	IM
08872	KX	C		IECA	GD
08873	KX		I	FXXL	SF
08874	KX	E		IECA	NL
08875	KX			RXLA	NL
08876	KX			DWCS	DR
08877	KX	C		DWCS	IM
08878	KX			FXXL	TI
	Grimesthorpe 41B				
08879	KX	C		RXLA	TI
	Earles				
08880	KX			FXXL	TI
	Mexborough 41F				
08881	KX			FGZZ	HA
08882	KX			FGZZ	AB
	Bennachie				
08883	KX			DBMS	ZH
08884	KX			FVZZ	AN
08885	KX			DWCS	DR
08886	KX			FXXL	GD
08887	KX			FGZZ	WN
08888	KX			IECA	GD
08889	KX			DWCS	CA
08890	KX			RXLA	WN
08891	KX			FXXL	LO
08892	BX			DBMS	ZG
08893	KX	C	F	FEZZ	BS
08894	KX			DCMB	SP
08895	KX	C		FXXL	LE
08896	KX			FXXL	LE
08897	KX			RXLA	LE
08898	KX			RXLA	LE
08899	KX			RXLA	DY
08900	KX			DWCS	BR
08901	KX			IWCA	BS
08902	KX			FVZZ	AN
08903	KX			FHZZ	DR
08904	KX			FGZZ	WN
08905	KX			FGZZ	WN
08906	KX			RXLA	TE
08907	KX		★	DWCS	CD
08908	KX			DWCS	NL
08909	KX			RXLA	BY
08910	KX			DWCS	CL
08911	KX			FGZZ	CL
08912	KX	C		FGZZ	CL
08913	KX			DWCS	CD
08914	KX			RXLA	BY
08915	KX			FXXL	LO
08916	KX			FPZZ	AN
08917	KX			FAZZ	AN
08918	KX			RXLA	AN
08919	KX	C		DWCS	TI
	Cadeby 41A				
08920	KX			FMZZ	BS
08921	KX			DWCS	CD
08922	KX			DCMB	BY
08923	KX			FXXL	SF
08924	KX			PXXA	AN
08925	KX			DCMB	SP
08926	KX			IWCA	WN
08927	KX			DCMB	BY
08928	KX	C	F	FXXL	TS
08929	BX			DWCS	AF
08930	KX			RXLA	SF
08931	KX			DWCS	GD
08932	KX			DWCS	CF
08933	BX			DWCS	EH
08934	KX			IWCA	WN
08935	KX			FGZZ	BR
08936	KX			DWCS	NC
08937	KX			FGZZ	LA
08938	KX	CR		FGZZ	ML
08939	KX			FGZZ	AN
08940	KX			FXXL	CF
08941	KX			DWCS	LA
08942	KX			DWCS	CF
08944	KX		★	RXLA	OC
08945	KX			FXXL	LA
08946	KX			FHZZ	RG
08947	KX			IXXA	OC
08948	KX	C		FGZZ	OC
08949	KX	C		IWRA	BR
08950	KX			RXLA	BR
08951	KX			RXLA	BR
08952	KX			FMZZ	ML

Loc No	Dia	SC	Liv	Pool	Dep
08953	KX			FGZZ	LA
	Plymouth				
08954	KX			FXXL	LA
	Penwithers				

Loc No	Dia	SC	Liv	Pool	Dep
08955	KX	c		RXLA	LA
08956	KX			FGZZ	NC
08957	KX			IECA	SF
08958	KX			FGZZ	SF

CLASS 08/9　　　SHUNTER　　　0-6-0

Built: British Rail 1958-59.
Details as Class 08/0 except height reduced to 11ft 10ins for operation of Cwm Mawr line (BPGV).

Diagram	Train Brake	Max Speed	Voltage
08-9CX	Dual	15mph	90
08-9DA	Air	15mph	90

Standard equipment: Refurbished cab (C), Headlight (L), and Sanding gear.

Sector:
Railfreight: **FHZZ:** Coal.

Loc No	Dia	SC	Liv	Pool	Dep	
08993	CX			FHZZ	LE	Ashburnham
08994	DA		F	FHZZ	LE	Gwendraeth
08995	DA		Fc	FHZZ	LE	Kidwelly

CLASS 09　　　SHUNTER　　　0-6-0

Built: British Rail 1959-62.
Engine: English Electric 6cyl, 4-stroke, 6KT of 400hp (315kW).
Weight: 50 tonnes.
Dimensions: 29.3ft L × 8.5ft W × 12.7ft H.
Brake force: 19 tonnes.
Maximum tractive effort: 25,000lb (112kN).

Power/control equipment: Two English Electric EE 506 traction motors; double reduction gear drive; main generator EE 801.
Route availability: 5.
Fuel: 668gal.
Train brakes: Dual Air and Vacuum.
Maximum operating speed: 27.5mph.
Diagram: 09-0AX.
Standard equipment: Sanding gear.

Sectors:
Departmental: **DCSB:** DCE Southern.
InterCity: **ICCA:** Cross Country. **IVGA:** Gatwick Express.
Network SouthEast: **NXXA:** General.
Railfreight: **FGZZ:** Distribution (Speedlink). **FMZZ:** Metals. **FXXL:** General.
Parcels: **RXLA:** General.
Special livery: *Light blue:* 09026.

Loc No	Dia	SC	Liv	Pool	Dep	Loc No	Dia	SC	Liv	Pool	Dep
09001		c		FGZZ	EH	09014				DCSB	SU
09002				RXLA	AF	09015		c		FGZZ	EH
09003		c		DCSB	SU	09016				NXXA	SU
09004				DCSB	SU	09018				FXXL	AF
09005		c		DCSB	SU	09019		c		DCSB	AF
09006				NXXA	SU	09020				ICCA	SU
09007				DCSB	SU	09021				DCSB	AF
09008				FMZZ	CF	09022		c		FGZZ	AF
09009				DCSB	SU	09023				NXXA	AF
09010		c		FGZZ	SU	09024				FGZZ	AF
09011		c		DCSB	AF	09025		c		FGZZ	EH
09012			I	IVGA	SU			Victory			
	Dick Hardy										
09013				FMZZ	CF	09026		c	★	DCSB	EH

CLASS 20	**TYPE 1**	**BO-BO**

Built: English Electric 1957-68.
Engine: English Electric 8cyl, 4-stroke, 8SVT Mk2 of 1,000hp (746kW).
Weight: 73-74 tonnes.
Dimensions: 46.8ft L × 8.8ft W × 12.6ft H.
Brake force: 35 tonnes.
Maximum tractive effort: 42,000lb (187kN).
Power/control equipment: Four English Electric traction motors (see below); main generator EE819/3C.
Route availability: 5.
Fuel: 380gal, except *SC 'x'* 1,040gal.
Maximum operating speed: 60mph (originally 75mph).

Standard equipment: AWS, Multiple working (Blue star), Guard's emergency brake, Sanding gear, Single cab.
Special characteristics: Slow speed control (s), Transponder code transmitter (t), Snowplough brackets (k), One man operation (m), Radio Electronic Token Block (r), Remote control radio, experimental (n), Headlight (cab front only) (l) as shown.

Diagram	Train Brake	Traction Motors
20-0BX	Dual	EE526/5D
20-0DX	Dual	EE526/8D
20-0FX	Dual	EE526/8D

18

Sectors:
Departmental: **DCEA:** DCE Eastern. **DCMA:** DCE Midland. **DWCQ:** DMEE, General.
Railfreight: **FEGA:** Coal, Fife. **FEND:** Coal, East Midlands. **FENW:** Coal, West Coast route (Crewe). **FGXX:** Distribution, General (Speedlink). **FMGA:** Metals (Steel), Glasgow. **FMYI:** Metals (Steel), Immingham. **FTYT:** Chemicals, Thornaby.
Special livery: *Green:* 20030/64.

Loc No	Dia	SC	Liv	Pool	Dep	Loc No	Dia	SC	Liv	Pool	Dep
20004	BX	STM		FENW	TO	20057	DX	SM		FENW	TO
20005	BX	SM		DCMA	TO	20058	DX	SMR		FENW	TO
20006	BX	STM		FENW	TO	20059	DX	SM	F	FEND	TO
20007	BX	SM		FENW	TO	20060	DX	SM		DCMA	TO
20008	BX			FTYT	TE	20061	DX	M		FMYI	IM
20009	BX	M		FPLI	IM	20063	DX	M		DCMA	TO
20010	BX	SM	F	FENW	TO	20064	DX	M	★	DCEA	IM
20013	BX	SM		FENW	TO	20065	DX	STM		FENW	TO
20016	BX	STM		FENW	TO	20066	DX	M		DWCQ	ED
20019	BX	SM		FENW	TO	20069	DX	M		FMYI	IM
20020	BX	STM		FENW	TO	20070	DX	SKM		DCMA	TO
20021	BX	SM		FENW	TO	20071	DX	SKM		FEND	TO
20023	BX	SM	F	FENW	TO	20072	DX	STKM		DCMA	TO
20025	BX	M		FMYI	IM	20073	DX	SKM		FENW	TO
20026	BX	STM		FEND	TO	20075	DX	SKM		FENW	TO
20028	BX	SM		FMYT	TE	20078	DX	SKM		FENW	TO
Bedale						20080	DX	STKM		FENW	TO
						20081	DX	STKM		FEND	TO
20029	BX	KM		DCMA	TO	20082	DX	STKM		FEND	TO
20030	BX	KM	★	DCEA	IM	20083	DX	STKM		FGXX	TO
20031	BX	KM		FMYI	IM	20084	DX	SXKM		FEND	TO
20032	BX	SKM		DCMA	TO	20085	DX	SKM		FEND	TO
20034	BX	SKM		DCMA	TO	20087	DX	SMKR		FENW	TO
20035	BX	M		FPLI	IM	20088	DX	SKM	F-	FEND	TO
20040	BX	SM		FENW	TO	20090	DX	SKM	F	FENW	TO
20041	BX	STM		DCMA	TO	20092	DX	KM		FMYI	IM
20042	BX	M		DCMA	TO	20093	DX	KM		FMYI	IM
20043	BX	M		FMYI	IM	20094	DX	SKM		FEND	TO
20044	BX	M		FMYI	IM	20095	DX	KM		FMYI	IM
20045	BX	SM		FENW	TO	20096	DX	KM		DCEA	IM
20046	BX	M		FMYI	IM	20097	DX	KM		DCMA	TO
20047	BX	SM		FEND	TO	20098	DX	KM		FMYI	IM
20048	BX	M		DCMA	TO	20099	DX	STKM		DCMA	TO
20051	DX	SM		FENW	TO	20100	DX	KM		FGXX	TO
20052	DX	STM		FENW	TO	20101	DX	STK		DCMA	TO
20053	DX	STM		FENW	TO	20102	DX	KM		FMYI	IM
20054	DX	M		DCMA	TO	20103	DX	SKM		FEND	TO
20055	DX	SM		FENW	TO	20104	DX	SKM	F	FEND	TO
20056	DX	SM		FENW	TO	20105	DX	STKM		FEND	TO

Loc No	Dia	SC	Liv	Pool	Dep
20106	DX	SKM		FENW	TO
20107	DX	KM		FMYI	IM
20108	DX	SKM	F	FEND	TO
20110	DX	KM		FMYI	IM
20112	DX	KM		FMYI	IM
20113	DX	STKM		FENW	TO
20114	DX	KMRL		DCHB	ED
20117	DX	SKM		FENW	TO
20118	DX	KM		FTYT	TE
Saltburn-on-the-Sea					
20119	DX	KM		FTYT	TE
20120	DX	SKM		FENW	TO
20121	DX	SKM		FENW	TO
20122	DX	KM	F	FTYT	TE
Cleveland Potash					
20124	DX	K		DCMA	TO
20126	DX	KM		FMYI	IM
20127	DX	KMRL		DCHB	ED
20128	DX	SKM		FEND	TO
20129	FX	SKM		FEND	TO
20130	FX	SKM		FENW	TO
20131	FX	SKM		FEND	TO
20132	FX	SKM	F	FENW	TO
20133	FX	SKM		FEND	TO
20134	FX	SKM		FEND	TO
20135	FX	SKM		FENW	TO
20136	FX	SKM		FEND	TO
20137	FX	KM	F	FTYT	TE
Murray B. Hofmeyr					
20138	FX	KMRL	F	DCHB	ED
20139	FX	K		DCMA	TO
20140	FX	SKM		FEND	TO
20141	FX	SKM	F	FENW	TO
20142	FX	SKM		FEND	TO
20143	FX	SKM		FENW	TO
20144	FX	K		FTYT	TE
20145	FX	KM		FPLI	IM
20146	FX	K		DWCQ	ED
20147	FX	SKM		DCMA	TO
20148	FX	KM		DWCQ	ED
20151	FX	SKM		FEND	TO
20154	FX	SKM		FEND	TO
20156	FX	KM	F	FTYT	TE
HMS Endeavour					
20157	FX	SKM		FEND	TO
20158	FX	SKM		DCMA	TO
20159	FX	SKM		FENW	TO
20160	FX	SK		DCMA	TO
20163	FX	SKM	F	FEND	TO
20165	FX	K	F	FTYT	TE
Henry Pease					
20166	FX	SKM		FEND	TO
20168	FX	SKM		FENW	TO
20169	FX	SKM		FENW	TO
20170	FX	SKM	F	FEND	TO
20171	FX	KM		FPLI	IM
20172	FX	SKM		FMYT	TE
Redmire					
20173	FX	SKM		FGXX	TO
20175	FX	SKM	F	FENW	TO
20176	FX	K		DCMA	TO
20177	FX	SKM		FEND	TO
20178	FX	SKM		FENW	TO
20179	FX	SKM	F	FEGA	ED
20182	FX	SKM		FEND	TO
20183	FX	SKM		FENW	TO
20185	FX	K		FGXX	IM
20186	FX	SKM		FEND	TO
20187	FX	SK		FEND	TO
20188	FX	SKM		FENW	TO
20189	FX	M		FGXX	TO
20190	FX	SKM		FEND	TO
20192	FX	SKM		FEGA	ED
20193	FX	SKM		FEGA	ED
20194	FX	SKM		FEND	TO
20195	FX	SK		DCMA	TO
20196	FX	SKM		FEND	TO
20197	FX	SKM		FENW	TO
20198	FX	SKM		FEGA	ED
20199	FX	SKM		FEGA	ED
20202	FX	SKM		DCEA	ED
20203	FX	SKM		FEGA	ED
20204	FX	SKM		DWCQ	ED
20205	FX	SKM		FEGA	ED
20206	FX	SKM		FEGA	ED
20208	FX	SKML		FEGA	ED
20209	FX	SK		DCMA	TO
20210	FX	SKM		FEND	TO
20211	FX	SKM		FEGA	ED

Loc No	Dia	SC	Liv	Pool	Dep	Loc No	Dia	SC	Liv	Pool	Dep
20212	FX	SKM		FEGA	ED	20219	FX	SKM		FGXX	TO
20213	FX	SKM		FEGA	ED	20224	FX	KM		FGXX	TO
20214	FX	SKM		FEND	TO	20225	FX	SKM		FGXX	TO
20215	FX	SKM	F	FEND	TO	20226	FX	KM		FPLI	IM
20217	FX	SKM		DCMA	TO	20227	FX	KM	F	DWCQ	ED
20218	FX	KM		FGXX	TO	20228	FX	KML		FGXX	IM

CLASS 26/0   TYPE 2   BO-BO

Built: Birmingham RC&W Ltd 1958-59.
Engine: Sulzer 6cyl, 4-stroke, 6LDA28B of 1,160hp (865kW).
Weight: 75-77 tonnes.
Dimensions: 50.8ft L × 8.8ft W × 12.7ft H.
Brake force: 35 tonnes.
Maximum tractive effort: 42,000lb (187kN).
Power/control equipment: Four Crompton Parkinson C171 A1 traction motors; main generator Crompton Parkinson CG391 A1.

Route availability: 6.
Fuel: 500gal.
Train brakes: Dual Air and Vacuum.
Maximum operating speed: 75mph.
Diagram: 26-0AX.
Standard equipment: Multiple working (Blue star), One man operation (M), Sanding gear.
Special characteristics: Slow speed control (s) as shown.

Sectors:
Departmental: **DCHA:** DCE Scottish Region. **DWCQ:** DMEE, General.
Railfreight: **FEGB:** Coal, Lothians.

Loc No	Dia	SC	Liv	Pool	Dep	Loc No	Dia	SC	Liv	Pool	Dep
26001	AX	s	F	FEGB	ED	26007	AX	s	F	FEGB	ED
26002	AX	s	F	FEGB	ED	26008	AX		F	FEGB	ED
26003	AX	s	F	FEGB	ED	26010	AX		F	DWCQ	ED
26004	AX	s	F	FEGB	ED	26011	AX			DCHA	ED
26005	AX	s	F	FEGB	ED	26014	AX			DCHA	ED
26006	AX	s	F	FEGB	ED	26015	AX			DCHA	ED

CLASS 26/1   TYPE 2   BO-BO

Built: Birmingham RC&W Ltd 1959.
Engine: Sulzer 6cyl, 4-stroke, 6LDA28B of 1,160hp (865kW).
Weight: 75 tonnes.

Dimensions: 50.8ft L × 8.8ft W × 12.7ft H.
Brake force: 35 tonnes.
Maximum tractive effort: 42,000lb (187kN).

Power/control equipment: Four Crompton Parkinson C171 A1 traction motors; main generator Crompton Parkinson CG391 A1.
Route availability: 5.
Fuel: 500gal.
Train brakes: Dual Air and Vacuum.

Maximum operating speed: 75mph.
Standard equipment: Multiple working (Blue Star), One man operation (m). Sanding gear, Snowplough brackets (k).
Diagram: 26-1CX.

Sectors:
Departmental: **DCHA:** DCE Scottish Region. **DWCQ:** DMEE, General.
Railfreight: **FGWS:** Distribution (Speedlink), Eastfield.

Loc No	Dia	SC	Liv	Pool	Dep		Loc No	Dia	SC	Liv	Pool	Dep
26021	DX			DCHA	ED		26035	DX		F	DCHA	ED
26023	DX			DCHA	ED		26036	DX			DCHA	ED
26024	DX			DCHA	ED		26037	DX		F	FGWS	ED
26025	DX		F	FGWS	ED		26038	DX		F	FGWS	ED
26026	DX		F	DCHA	ED		26039	DX			DCHA	ED
26027	DX			DCHA	ED		26040	DX		F	FGWS	ED
26028	DX			DCHA	ED		26041	DX		F	FGWS	ED
26031	DX		F	FGWS	ED		26042	DX			DWCQ	ED
26032	DX		F	FGWS	ED		26043	DX			DWCQ	ED
26034	DX		F	FGWS	ED		26046	DX			DWCQ	ED

CLASS 31/1   TYPE 2   A1A-A1A

Built: Brush Traction 1959-62.
Engine: English Electric 12cyl, 4-stroke, 12SVT of 1,470hp (1,097kW).
Weight: 49 tonnes.
Dimensions: 56.8ft L × 8.8ft W × 12.6ft H.
Power/control equipment: Four Brush traction motors TM73-68, main generator Brush TG160-48.
Route availability: 5.
Fuel: 530gal except *SC* 'x' 1,230gal.
Train brake: Dual Air and Vacuum.
Maximum operating speed: 75mph.
(Diagram 31-1GX originally 80mph, others 90mph).

Train heating: Not operational. (Diagram 31-1CX retains Spanner Swirlyflow Mk 1 1,500lb/hr steam generator isolated and 100gal boiler fuel tank.)
Water tank: 600gal.
Standard equipment: AWS, Multiple Working (Blue star), One man operation (м), Sanding gear.
Special characteristics: Snowplough brackets (к), Headlight (ʟ) as shown.

Diagram	Weight	Maximum Tractive Effort	
31-1CX	111 tonnes	35,900lb	(Boiler fitted)
31-1FX	108 tonnes	35,900lb	
31-1GX	108 tonnes	42,800lb	

Sectors:
Departmental: **DCAA:** DCE Anglia. **DCEA:** DCE Eastern. **DCMA:** DCE Midland. **DWCQ:** DMEE General.
Railfreight: **FALG:** Construction, Stone, Stratford. **FAMA:** Construction, Stone, Thornaby. **FGWC:** Distribution (Speedlink), Tinsley. **FHHA:** Flask, Crewe. **FPLI:** Petroleum, Immingham. **FTLC:** Chemicals, Crewe.

Loc No	Dia	SC	Liv	Pool	Dep	Loc No	Dia	SC	Liv	Pool	Dep
31101	FX			DWCQ	IM	31160	FX	LK	F	FGWC	TI
31102	FX	L	F	FGWC	TI	31162	CX			DCMA	BS
31105	GX		F	DWCQ	SF	31163	FX		F	FGWC	TI
31106	GX			DWCQ	BS	31164	FX	LK	F	FGWC	TI
31107	FX		F	DCMA	BS	31165	FX			DCAA	SF
31108	FX		F	FGWC	TI	31166	FX		F	FGWC	TI
31110	FX		F	FGWC	TI	31168	CX			DCMA	BS
31112	GX		F	DCMA	BS	31170	CX			DCEA	IM
31113	FX		F	FGWC	TI	31171	FX	L	F	FGWC	TI
31116	FX	L	F	FALG	SF	31173	CX			DCAA	SF
31118	FX	K		DCEA	TE	31174	FX		F	FGWC	TI
31119	FX		F	DCMA	BS	31178	FX		F	DCMA	BS
31120	FX	K	F	FHHA	CD	31180	FX		F	FGWC	TI
31123	FX	K		DCEA	TE	31181	FX		F	DCAA	SF
31124	FX			DCMA	BS	31184	FX	L	F	FAMA	TE
31125	FX	K	F	FGWC	TI	31185	FX		F	FPLI	IM
31126	FX	LK	F	FGWC	TI	31186	FX		F	DCAA	SF
31127	CX			DCAA	SF	31187	FX		F	DCAA	SF
31128	FX		F	FALG	SF	31188	FX		F	FPLI	IM
31130	FX	L	F	FHHA	CD	31189	CX			DWCQ	SF
31131	CX			DWCQ	TE	31190	FX		F	DCAA	SF
31132	FX	LK	F	FGWC	TI	31191	FX		F	DCAA	SF
31134	FX		F	FALG	SF	31196	FX		F	DWCQ	IM
31135	FX		F	DWCQ	BS	31198	FX		F	FALG	SF
31138	FX			DCMA	BS	31199	FX		F	FPLI	IM
31141	FX			DCMA	BS	31200	FX	K	F	FHHA	CD
31142	FX	K	F	FGWC	TI	31201	FX		F	FPLI	IM
31143	FX		F	FGWC	TI	31203	FX	L	F	FPLI	IM
31144	FX		F	FGWC	TI	31205	FX		F	DWCQ	IM
31145	FX		F	FGWC	TI	31206	FX			DWCQ	IM
31146	FX	LK	F	FGWC	TI	31207	FX	L	F	FPLI	IM
31147	FX		F	FGWC	TI	31208	CX			DCEA	IM
31149	FX		F	DCMA	BS	31209	FX		F	FALG	SF
31152	CX			DCMA	BS	31210	FX	K	F	FPLI	IM
31154	FX		F	FPLI	IM	31212	CX			FPLI	IM
31155	FX		F	FGWC	TI	31215	FX		F	FAMA	TE
31156	FX			FPLI	IM	31217	FX		F	FHHA	CD
31158	FX		F	FGWC	TI	31219	FX		F	DCAA	SF
31159	FX		F	FGWC	TI	31221	FX			DCEA	IM

Loc No	Dia	SC	Liv	Pool	Dep
31223	CX			FPLI	IM
31224	FX		F	DCAA	SF
31225	CX			FPLI	IM
31226	FX		F	FALG	SF
31227	FX			FPLI	IM
31229	FX	LK	F	FAMA	TE
31230	GX	L	F	DWCQ	BS
31231	CX			DCAA	SF
31232	FX		F	DWCQ	IM
31233	FX		F	FPLI	IM
31234	FX		F	FALG	SF
31235	FX		F	DCMA	BS
31237	FX		F	DCMA	BS
31238	FX		F	FPLI	IM
31240	FX		F	FALG	SF
31242	FX		F	DCEA	IM
31243	FX		F	FPLI	IM
31247	FX		F	DCEA	IM
31248	FX		F	FGWC	TI
31249	CX			FPLI	IM
31250	FX		F	DCAA	SF
31252	FX		F	DWCQ	BS
31255	FX		F	DWCQ	BS
31257	CX			DCMA	BS
31259	CX	K		FGWC	TI
31260	FX			DWCQ	TE
31263	FX		F	DCAA	SF
31264	CX			DWCQ	TE
31268	FX		F	DCAA	SF
31270	FX	LK	F	FHHA	CD
31271	FX	K	F	DCMA	BS
31272	FX		F	DWCQ	SF
31273	FX	K	F	FPLI	IM
31275	FX	K	F	FHHA	CD
31276	FX		F	FHHA	CD

Calder Hall Power Station

Loc No	Dia	SC	Liv	Pool	Dep
31278	FX			DCEA	TE
31281	FX			DCEA	TE
31282	FX		F	DCEA	TE
31283	FX			DCEA	TE
31284	FX			DCEA	TE
31285	FX		F	DCEA	TE
31286	CX			DWCQ	TE
31288	FX			DCMA	BS
31289	FX			DCMA	BS
31290	FX	L	F	DWCQ	BS
31292	FX			DWCQ	BS
31293	CX			DCMA	BS
31294	FX	K	F	FALG	SF
31296	FX	L		DCMA	BS

Trên Nwyddau Amlwch, Amlwch Freighter

Loc No	Dia	SC	Liv	Pool	Dep
31299	FX		F	FPLI	IM
31301	FX		F	DCMA	BS
31302	FX		F	FPLI	IM
31304	FX	LK	F	FPLI	IM
31305	CX			DCMA	BS
31306	FX	L	F	FALG	SF
31308	FX		F	FALG	SF
31309	CX			LNRD	TI

Cricklewood

Loc No	Dia	SC	Liv	Pool	Dep
31311	FX			DCMA	BS
31312	FX	K	F	FHHA	CD
31317	FX	LK	F	DCMA	BS
31319	FX	LK	F	FPLI	IM
31320	FX			DCAA	SF
31322	FX			DCMA	BS
31323	CX			DWCQ	SF
31324	FX		F	FHHA	CD
31327	FX		F	FALG	SF

Phillips-Imperial

CLASS 31/4 — TYPE 2 — A1A-A1A

Built: Brush Traction 1959-62.
Engine: English Electric 12cyl, 4-stroke, 12SVT of 1,470hp (1,097kW).

Brake force: 49 tonnes.
Maximum tractive effort: 35,900lb.
Dimensions: 56.8ft L × 8.8ft W × 12.6ft H.

Power/control equipment: Four Brush traction motors TM73-68, main generator Brush TG160-48.
Route availability: 5.
Fuel: 530gal.
Train brake: Dual Air and Vacuum.
Maximum operating speed: 90mph.
Train heating: Brush electric alternator BL100-30 driven by main engine 320kW.
ETH Index: 66.

Water tanks: 600gal.
Standard equipment: AWS, Multiple working (Blue star), One man operation (M), Sanding gear.
Special characteristics: Headlights (L) as shown.

Diagram	Weight
31-4CX	109 tonnes

Sectors:
Departmental: **DCEA:** DCE Eastern. **DCMA:** DCE Midland. **DCQA:** DCE BRB HQ. **DWCQ:** DMEE General.
Railfreight: **FGWC:** Distribution (Speedlink), Tinsley. **FPLI:** Petroleum, Immingham.
Provincial: **PXXA:** General.
Parcels: **RXLB:** General.
Special livery: Dark blue 31413/430

Loc No	Dia	SC	Liv	Pool	Dep		Loc No	Dia	SC	Liv	Pool	Dep
31400	CX			RXLB	CD		31426	CX			DCQA	CD
31402	CX			FGWC	TI		31427	CX			RXLB	CD
31403	CX			DCWA	OC		31428	CX			RXLB	CD
31404	CX			RXLB	CD		*North Yorkshire Moors Railway*					
31405	CX	L		RXLB	CD							
31406	CX	.		RXLB	CD		31429	CX			RXLB	CD
31407	CX			RXLB	CD		31430	CX		★	DCMA	BS
31408	CX			RXLB	CD		*Sister Dora*					
31409	CX			RXLB	CD							
31410	CX			RXLB	CD		31431	CX			DCEA	IM
31411	CX			DCMA	CD		31432	CX			DCEA	IM
31412	CX	L		DCQA	CD		31433	CX			DCMA	BS
31413	CX		★	DWCQ	BS		31434	CX			DCMA	BS
Severn Valley Railway							31435	CX			DCMA	BS
							31437	CX			DCMA	BS
31414	CX	L		DCQA	CD		31438	CX			RXLB	CD
31415	CX			DWCQ	BS		31439	CX			DCEA	IM
31416	CX			DCQA	CD		31441	CX			DCEA	IM
31417	CX			DWCQ	BS		31442	CX			RXLB	CD
31418	CX			RXLB	CD		31443	CX			RXLB	CD
31419	CX			RXLB	CD		31444	CX			DCEA	IM
31420	CX			DCMA	BS		*Keighley and Worth Valley Railway*					
31421	CX			RXLB	CD							
31422	CX			RXLB	CD		31445	CX			DCMA	BS
31423	CX	L		RXLB	CD		31446	CX			DCMA	BS
31424	CX			RXLB	CD		31447	CX	L		DCEA	IM
31425	CX			RXLB	CD		31448	CX	L		RXLB	CD

Loc No	Dia	SC	Liv	Pool	Dep	Loc No	Dia	SC	Liv	Pool	Dep
31449	CX	L		DCEA	IM	31460	CX			DCEA	IM
31450	CX	L		RXLB	CD	31461	CX			DWCQ	IM
31451	CX	L		RXLB	CD	31462	CX			DCWA	OC
31452	CX	L		DCEA	IM	31463	CX			DCWA	OC
31453	CX	L		DCEA	IM	31464	CX			RXLB	CD
31454	CX	L		RXLB	CD	31465	CX			DWCQ	BS
31455	CX	L		RXLB	CD	31466	CX			FGWC	TI
31456	CX			DCEA	IM	31467	CX			FGWC	TI
31457	CX			DWCQ	IM	31468	CX			DCMA	CD
31458	CX			DCEA	IM	31469	CX	L		DCEA	IM
31459	CX			RXLB	CD						

CLASS 33/0   TYPE 3   BO-BO

Built: Birmingham RC&W Ltd 1960-62.
Engine: Sulzer 8cyl, 4-stroke, 8LDA28 of 1,550hp (1,156kW).
Weight: 77 tonnes.
Dimensions: 50.8ft L × 9.3ft W × 12.7ft H.
Brake force: 35 tonnes.
Maximum tractive effort: 45,000lb.
Power/control equipment: Four Crompton Parkinson C171C2 traction motors; main generator Crompton Parkinson CG391B1.
Route availability: 6.
Fuel: 750gal.
Train brake: Dual Air and Vacuum.

Maximum operating speed: 85mph.
Train heating: Electric generator Crompton Parkinson CAG392A1 driven by engine, 235kW at 750V dc for heating only Mk 1, Mk 2a, b, c, d stock. SC 'u': Not maintained in working order.
ETH Index: 48 (except SC 'u').
Diagram: 33-OAX.
Standard equipment: Multiple working (blue star), One man operation (M), Snowplough brackets (K), Sanding gear.
Special characteristic: Train heating isolated (u).

Sectors:
Departmental: DCSA: Civil Engineer, Southern.
Railfreight: FALS: Construction, Stone, Southern. FPXX: Petroleum, General. FXXA: General.
Network SouthEast: NSSB: Solent and Sarum.
Special livery: Green: 33008.

Loc No	Dia	SC	Liv	Pool	Dep	Loc No	Dia	SC	Liv	Pool	Dep
33002	AX	u		DCSA	EH	33011	AX			FALS	SL
33004	AX			DCSA	SL	33012	AX			FALS	EH
33006	AX			DCSA	EH	33013	AX	u		DCSA	EH
33008	AX		★	FALS	EH	33015	AX			DCSA	EH
	Eastleigh					33016	AX			FALS	SL
						33019	AX			FXXA	SL
33009	AX			FALS	EH	33020	AX			FALS	EH

Loc No	Dia	SC	Liv	Pool	Dep
33021	AX		Fa	FALS	SL
33022	AX			FALS	SL
33023	AX			DCSA	EH
33025	AX			DCSA	EH
33026	AX			DCSA	EH
33027	AX			FALS	SL
Earl Mountbatten of Burma					
33029	AX			FALS	SL
33030	AX			DCSA	EH
33031	AX			FALS	SL
33033	AX			FALS	SL
33035	AX			FXXA	SL
33039	AX			FXXA	SL
33040	AX			FALS	SL
33042	AX	U		FALS	SL
33046	AX	U		FXXA	SL
33047	AX	U		FALS	SL
33048	AX			DCSA	SL
33050	AX		Fa	FALS	SL
Isle of Grain					

Loc No	Dia	SC	Liv	Pool	Dep
33051	AX		Fa	FALS	SL
Shakespeare Cliff					
33052	AX			FXXA	SL
Ashford					
33053	AX		Fa	FALS	SL
33055	AX			FALS	SL
33056	AX	U	Fa	FALS	SL
The Burma Star					
33057	AX	U		FALS	SL
33058	AX			FXXA	SL
33060	AX			FALS	SL
33063	AX	U		FXXA	SL
33064	AX		Fa	DCSA	EH
33065	AX			DCSA	EH

CLASS 33/1 — TYPE 3 — BO-BO

Specification as Class 33/0 above except as follows:
Built: 1960-61.
Weight: 78 tonnes.
Diagram: 33-1AX.
Standard equipment (additional): Buck-eye couplings (E), Flashlight adaptor (for Weymouth Quay line).

Special Characteristics: Push-Pull cabling for working in multiple with Buck-eye coupling fitted dc EMUs and Class 438 stock (P).

Sectors:
Departmental: **DCSA:** Civil Engineer, Southern.
Network SouthEast: **NSSB:** Solent and Sarum.
Parcels: **RXLA:** General.

Loc No	Dia	SC	Liv	Pool	Dep
33101	AX	P		NSSB	EH
33102	AX	PU		NSSB	EH
33103	AX	P		NSSB	EH
33106	AX	P		NSSB	EH

Loc No	Dia	SC	Liv	Pool	Dep
33107	AX	U		DCSA	EH
33108	AX	P		RXLC	EH
33109	AX	P		RXLC	EH
33110	AX	PU		DCSA	EH

Loc No	Dia	SC	Liv	Pool	Dep
33111	AX	P		RXLC	EH
33113	AX	P		RXLC	EH
33114	AX	P		NSSB	EH
Sultan					
33115	AX	P		RXLC	EH

Loc No	Dia	SC	Liv	Pool	Dep
33116	AX	P		RXLC	EH
33117	AX	P		DCSA	EH
33118	AX	P		DCSA	EH
33119	AX	P		RXLC	EH

CLASS 33/2   TYPE 3   BO-BO

Specification as Class 33/0 above except as follows:
Built: 1962.
Weight: 77 tonnes.

Dimensions: 50.8ft L × 8.7ft W × 12.7ft H.
Diagram: 33-2AX.
Standard equipment (additional): Slow speed control.(s).

Sectors:
Departmental: **DCSA:** Civil Engineer, Southern.
Railfreight: **FALS:** Construction, Stone, Southern. **FGWD:** Distribution (Speedlink), Dover Linkspan.
Footnote: 33205 was numbered 33302 for a few months during 1988.

Loc No	Dia	SC	Liv	Pool	Dep
33201	AX			DCSA	SL
33203	AX		FG	FGWD	SL
33204	AX			DCSA	SL
33205	AX		FG	FGWD	SL
33206	AX		FG	FGWD	SL

Loc No	Dia	SC	Liv	Pool	Dep
33207	AX			DCSA	SL
33208	AX			FALS	SL
33209	AX			DCSA	SL
33211	AX			FALS	SL

CLASS 37/0   TYPE 3   CO-CO

Built: English Electric 1960-65.
Engine: English Electric 12cyl, 4-stroke, 12CSVT of 1,750hp (1,306kW).
Weight: see below.
Dimensions: 61.5ft L × 8.8ft W *Height:* First series 12.9ft (except *SC* 'h'), Second series 13.1ft.
Brake force: 50 tonnes.
Maximum tractive effort: 55,500lb (247kN).
Power/control equipment: Six English Electric traction motors EE538/A; main generator EE Type 822/10G.

Train heating: Not operational. (Some retain Clayton RO2500 Steam General, 2,500lb/hr, isolated and 800gal water tank — see below.)
Train brakes: Dual air and vacuum.
Route availability: 5.
Fuel: see below.
Maximum operating speed: 80mph (originally 90 mph).
Standard equipment: AWS, Multiple working (Blue star), One man operation (M), Sanding gear.

Special characteristics: Radio electronic token block (R), Snowplough brackets (K), Headlight or spotlight (L), Revised height 13.1ft (H) as shown.

First series built with end doors and two part route indicator boxes, some since replaced with sealed end and two marker lights. Second series built with electrical variations, four character route indicator boxes, now used for marker lights, and roof mounted horns.

Diagram	Series	Weight	Fuel
37-0CX	First	105 tonnes	890gal*
37-0DX	First	103 tonnes	890gal
37-0EX	Second	105 tonnes	890gal
37-0GX	Second	107 tonnes	890gal*
37-0JX	Second	106 tonnes	1,690gal
37-0KX	Second	108 tonnes	1,690gal

*Steam generator fitted.

Sectors:

Departmental: **DCAA:** DCE Anglia. **DCHA:** DCE Scotland. **DCWA:** DCE Western.

Railfreight: **FEGA:** Coal, Fife. **FGWB:** Distribution (Speedlink), Tinsley. **FGXX:** Distribution (Speedlink), General. **FMCA:** Metals (Steel) Cardiff. **FMCH:** Metals (Steel), Cardiff (for HGR at Crewe Works). **FMGM:** Metals (Ore) Hunterston. **FMYI:** Metals (Steel), Immingham. **FMYT:** Metals, Thornaby. **FPGE:** Petroleum and Chemicals, Eastfield. **FPLW:** Petroleum, South Wales. **FQLC:** Distribution (Speedlink), Coal, Cardiff.

Freightliner: **LNRA:** General, Stratford.

Renumbering note: Locomotives 37310-26 are in the process of reverting to former numbers as follows: 37310 = 37152, 37311 = 37156, 37312 = 37137, 37313 = 37145, 37314 = 37190, 37320 = 37026, 37321 = 37037, 37322 = 37049, 37323 = 37088, 37324 = 37099, 37325 = 37108, 37326 = 37111.

Locomotives 37303, 37304, 37306 and 37308 will also be renumbered to Nos 37271-74 respectively.

Loc No	Dia	SC	Liv	Pool	Dep		Loc No	Dia	SC	Liv	Pool	Dep
37002	JX	XL	F	FMYI	IM		37048	DX			FMYI	IM
37003	JX	x		FGWB	TI		37049	CX			FMGM	ML
37004	DX			LNRA	SF			*Imperial*				
37009	JX	x		FGWB	TI							
37010	DX			FMGM	ML		37050	CX			FMCH	CF
37012	CX	K		LNRA	SF		37051	CX	K		FMGM	ML
37013	JX	x		FGWB	TI		37053	DX			LNRA	SF
37015	JX	XL		FGWB	TI		37054	CX			FMYI	IM
37019	DX			LNRA	SF		37055	DX			LNRA	SF
37023	DX			DCHA	ED		37057	DX			LNRA	SF
37025	CX	K		DCHA	ED		37058	JX	x		FGWB	TI
37026							37059	JX	x	FG	LNRA	TI
37029	JX	x		FGWB	TI			*Port of Tilbury*				
37031	JX	XK		FGWB	TI							
37035	CX	K		FPGE	ED		37062	JX	x		FGWB	TI
37037							37063	JX	x		FGWB	TI
37038	DX			LNRA	SF		37065	JX	x		FGWB	TI
37040	DX			FMGM	ML		37066	JX	x		FGWB	TI
37042	JX	x		FMYI	IM		37069	JX	x	F-	FMYT	TE
37046	DX			FMYT	TE			*Thornaby TMD*				
37047	CX			LNRA	SF							

Loc No	Dia	SC	Liv	Pool	Dep
37070	DX		FG	FGXX	IS
37071	JX	x		FGWB	TI
37072	JX	x		FGWB	TI
37073	JX	Xh		FGWB	TI
37074	DX	h		LNRA	SF
37075	DX		F-	FGWB	SF
37077	DX	K		LNRA	SF
37078	JX	x		FPLW	CF
37080	DX			FPGE	ED
37083	JX	x		FMYI	IM
37087	CX			LNRA	SF
37088					
37092	CX			FMGM	ML
37095	JX	x		FGWB	TI
37096	JX	x		FGWB	TI
37097	DX			DCHA	ED
37098	JX	x		FGWB	TI
37099					
37100	JX			LNRA	SF
37101	JX	x		FGWB	TI
37104	DX		Fx	LNRA	SF
37106	JX	x		FMYI	IM
37107	CX			LNRA	SF
37108					
37109	CX			FGXX	IS
37110	CX			FGXX	IS
37111					
37113	DX			FPGE	ED
37114	CX	TLK		FGXX	IS
Dunrobin Castle					
37116	CX			LNRA	SF
37128	EX	K		LNRA	SF
37131	KX	x		FQLC	CF
37133	EX			DCWA	CF
37137					
37138	EX	TL		FALG	SF
37139	KX	x		FQLC	CF
37140	EX	TL		DCAA	SF
37141	EX			DCWA	CF
37142	EX			DCWA	CF
37144	EX	TL		FALG	SF
37145					
37146	EX			DCWA	CF
37152					
37153	EX	K		DCHA	IS
37154	EX	K		LNRA	SF

Loc No	Dia	SC	Liv	Pool	Dep
37156					
37158	EX	K		DCWA	CF
37162	KX	x		FQLC	CF
37167	KX	x		FQLC	CF
37170	EX	K		DCHA	ED
37174	EX	K		DCWA	CF
37175	EX	LK		DCHA	IS
37178	GX	K		LNRA	SF
37184	GX	K		FPGE	ED
37185	KX	XK		FGWB	TI
37188	GX	LK		FPGE	ED
Jimmy Shand					
37190	GX	LK		FMGM	ML
Dalzell					
37191	GX	LK		FPGE	ED
37194	KX	XK		FGWB	TI
37196	EX	K	F	FGXX	IS
37197	KX	XK		FMCA	CF
37198	KX	XK		FGWB	TI
37201	EX	K		FMGM	ML
37202	EX	K		FMYI	IM
37203	EX	K		FMYI	IM
37207	EX	K		DCWA	CF
37209	EX	K		LNRA	SF
37211	EX	K		FAWC	CF
37212	KX	XK		FQLC	CF
37213	KX	K		FQLC	CF
37214	KX	XK		FQLC	CF
37215	EX	K		DCWA	CF
37216	KX	XTLK		DCAA	SF
37217	KX	XK		FQLC	CF
37218	EX	K		FAWC	CF
37219	EX	TLK		FALG	SF
37220	KX	XK		FPLW	CF
37221	EX	K		FQLC	SF
37222	KX	XK		FQLC	CF
37223	KX	XK		FQLC	CF
37225	KX	XK		FMYI	IM
37227	KX	XK		FQLC	CF
37229	KX	XK	F-	FEGA	ED
37230	KX	XK		FQLC	CF
37232	EX	K		FPGE	ED
37235	KX	XK		FQLC	CF
Coal Merchants' Association of Scotland					

Loc No	Dia	SC	Liv	Pool	Dep
37238	EX	K		LNRA	SF
37239	KX	XK		FQLC	CF
37240	KX	XK		FEGA	ED
37241	EX	K		FMYI	IM
37242	KX	XK		FGWB	TI
37244	KX	XK		FQLC	CF
37245	K	K		FPGE	ED
37248	KX	XK		FPLW	CF
37250	KX	XK	F	FEGA	ED
37251	KX	XK		FGWB	TI
37252	EX	K		LNRA	SF
37254	KX	XK		FMCA	CF
37255	KX	XK	F	FMYI	IM
37258	KX	XK		FMYI	IM
37260	GX	TLK		FGXX	IS
	Radio Highland				
37261	GX	TLK		DCHA	IS
	Caithness				
37262	GX	TLK		DCHA	IS
	Dounreay				
37263	GX	K		DCWA	CF
37264	GX	LK		DCWA	CF
37275	KX	XK		FMYI	IM
37278	KX	XK		FMCA	CF
37280	KX	XK		FPLW	CF
37285	KX	XK	F-	FGWB	TI
37293	KX	XK		FMCA	CF
37294	KX	X		FQLC	CF
37298	KX	XK		FGWB	TI

Loc No	Dia	SC	Liv	Pool	Dep
37303	KX	XK		FGWB	TI
37304	KX	XK		FGWB	TI
37306	KX	XK		FPLW	CF
37308	KX	K		FQLC	CF
37310	EX	K		FMGM	ML
	British Steel Ravenscraig				
37311	EX	K		FMGM	ML
	British Steel Hunterston				
37312	EX			FMGM	ML
	Clyde Iron				
37313	EX			FMGM	ML
37320	KX	XLK		FMGM	ML
	Shap Fell				
37321	CX	LK		FMGM	ML
	Gartcosh				
37323	CX	L		FMGM	ML
	Clydesdale				
37324	CX	L		FMGM	ML
	Clydebridge				
37325	CX	LK		FMGM	ML
	Lanarkshire Steel				
37326	CX	K		FMGM	ML
	Glengarnock				

CLASS 37/3   TYPE 3   CO-CO

Specification as Class 37/0 but fitted with refurbished bogies during 1987/88 at BREL Crewe.

Diagram	Series	Weight	Fuel
37-3AX	First	103 tonnes	890gal
37-3BX	First	106 tonnes	1,690gal
37-3CX	Second	105 tonnes	890gal
37-3DX	Second	108 tonnes	1,690gal

Sectors:
Departmental: **DCWA:** DCE Western Region.
Railfreight: **FAMM:** Construction (Stone), Motherwell. **FAMT:** Construction (Stone), Tinsley. **FGWB:** Distribution (Speedlink), Tinsley. **FMYI:** Metals (Steel) Immingham. **FPLX:** Petroleum, North Thames, Ripple Lane. **FQLC:** Distribution (Speedlink), Coal, Cardiff.
Special livery: *Green:* 37350.

Loco No	Former No	Dia	SC	Liv	Pool	Dep		Loc No	Former No	Dia	SC	Liv	Pool	Dep
37350	(37119)	BX	x	★	FPLX	SF		37370	(37127)	CX		F	FAMM	ML
37351	(37002)							37371	(37147)	DX	x	F	FPLW	CF
37352	(37008)	BX	x	F	FGWB	TI		37372	(37159)	CX		F	DCWA	CF
37353	(37032)	BX	x	F	FGWB	TI		37373	(37160)	CX		F	FAMM	ML
37354	(37043)	AX	K	Fa	FALG	SF		37374	(37165)	DX		F	FQLC	CF
37355	(37045)	BX	x	F	FGWB	TI		37375	(37193)	DX		F	FQLC	CF
37356	(37068)	BX	x	F	FGWB	TI		37376	(37199)	DX	XK	F	FQLC	CF
	Grainflow							37377	(37200)	DX	XK	F	FMYI	IM
								37378	(37204)	DX	XK	F	FGWB	TI
37357	(37079)	BX	x	F	FGWB	TI		37379	(37226)	CX	K	F	FAMM	ML
37358	(37091)	AX			LNRA	SF		37380	(37259)	CX	K	F-	FAMT	TI
	P & O Containers							37381	(37284)	DX	XK	FM	FMYI	IM
37359	(37118)	CX	L	F	FPGE	ED								

CLASS 37/4   TYPE 3   CO-CO

Built: English Electric 1965, ETH fitted 1985/86.
Engine: as Class 37/0.
Weight: 107 tonnes.
Dimensions: as Class 37/0 Second series.
Brake force, Maximum tractive effort, Train brakes, Route availability, Maximum operating speed: As Class 37/0.
Power/control equipment: Six English Electric traction motors EE538/A, main alternator Brush BA100SA.

Train heating: Electric, Brush alternator BAH 701.
ETH Index: 30.
Fuel: 1,689gal.
Diagram: 37-4AX.
Standard equipment: AWS, Headlight (L), Multiple working (Blue star), One man operation (M), Sanding gear, Snowplough brackets (K).
Special characteristics: Radio Electronic Token Block (R).

Sectors:
Departmental: **DCHA:** DCE Scotland.
Railfreight: **FAWC:** Construction (Stone), Cardiff. **FGXX:** Distribution (Speedlink), General. **FMGA:** Metals, Glasgow.
InterCity: **ICHA:** Charter. **IWCA:** West Coast main line.
Provincial: **PXXA:** General.

Class 08 0-6-0 No 08770 is seen carrying Railfreight livery, with No 08867 *Ralph Easby* behind. *Thomas Silsbury*

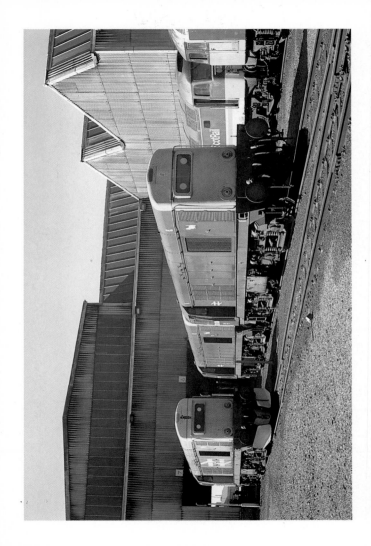

Eastfield TMD plays host to Class 20 B0-B0s Nos 20206, 20138 (in Railfreight livery) and 20211 on 12 June 1988.
Hugh Ballantyne

Class 26/1 Bo-Bo No 26021 is seen at Eastfield TMD on 12 June 1988. *Hugh Ballantyne*

Class 31/1 A1A-A1A No 31196 still carried 'red stripe' Railfreight livery when it was photographed at Bristol Temple Meads on 22 December 1987.   *John Chalcraft*

Class 33/2 Bo-Bo No 33205 in Railfreight livery. *Brian Morrison*

Class 37/5 Co-Co No 37507 *BSC Hartlepool Pipe Mill* displays the latest Railfreight livery with Metals & Automotives sub-Sector symbols at Thornaby on 18 February 1988. *Barry Nicolle*

Class 45/1 'Peak' 1Co-Co1 No 45106 is retained by the InterCity Sector for charter work, and is seen here at Wigan Springs Branch on 18 September 1988. The locomotive has been repainted in green livery, although the large nose-end numerals have since been painted out. *Hugh Ballantyne*

Class 47/0 No 47079 in Railfreight livery

The unique Class 50/1 Co-Co No 50149 *Defiance* passes Golant with a china clay working to Carne Point on 4 May 1988.
Hugh Ballantyne

Class 56 CO-CO No 56001 at Stratford. *John Augustson*

Model of the forthcoming Class 60 heavy freight locomotive. *Courtesy of Brush Traction*

Class 73/0 electro-diesel No 73004 *The Bluebell Railway* at Basingstoke on 5 April 1988. The Mid-Hants Railway has since been commemorated on No 73005. *John Chalcraft*

Class 86/2 B0-B0 No 86235 *Novelty* on display at Ripple Lane on 17 October 1987.   *John Augustson*

Class 90 B0-B0 No 90005 is stabled in Platform 10 at Crewe station between test workings on 10 August 1988.   *Kieran J. Platt*

One of the star attractions at Bescot open day on 9 October 1988 was immaculately-preserved Class 52 'Western' C-C No D1041 *Western Prince*. *John Robinson*

HST power car No 43004, in the latest InterCity 'Swallow' livery with enlarged yellow end panel, passes Aller Junction with the 14.30 Penzance-Paddington on 9 August 1988. *Peter J. Robinson*

Loc No	Dia	SC	Liv	Pool	Dep	Name
37401	AX	RK	I	IWCA	ED	Mary Queen of Scots
37402	AX	RK		DCHA	ED	Oor Wullie
37403	AX	RK		PXXA	ED	Glendarroch
37404	AX	RK		FGXX	ED	Ben Cruachan
37405	AX	RK		PXXA	ED	Strathclyde Region
37406	AX	RK		FGXX	ED	The Saltire Society
37407	AX	RK		PXXA	ED	Loch Long
37408	AX	RK		PXXA	ED	Loch Rannoch
37409	AX	RK		ICHA	ED	Loch Awe
37410	AX	RK		FGXX	ED	Aluminium 100
37411	AX	RK		PXXA	ED	Institution of Railway Signal Engineers
37412	AX	RK		PXXA	ED	Loch Lomond
37413	AX	RK		FGXX	ED	Loch Eil Outward Bound
37414	AX	RK		PXXA	IS	
37415	AX	RK		PXXA	IS	
37416	AX	RK		PXXA	IS	
37417	AX	RK		PXXA	IS	Highland Region
37418	AX	RK		PXXA	IS	An Comunn Gaidhealach
37419	AX	RK		PXXA	IS	
37420	AX	RK		PXXA	IS	The Scottish Hosteller
37421	AX	RK		PXXA	IS	
37422	AX	RK		DCHA	ED	
37423	AX	RK	FM	FMGA	ED	Sir Murray Morrison 1874-1948
37424	AX	RK		ICHA	ED	Isle of Mull
37425	AX	RK		PXXA	ED	Sir Robert MacAlpine, Concrete Bob
37426	AX	K		FAWC	CF	Y Lein Fach, Vale of Rheidol
37427	AX	RK		PXXA	CF	Bont Y Bermo
37428	AX	RK		PXXA	CF	David Lloyd George
37429	AX	RK		PXXA	CF	Eisteddfod Genedlaethol
37430	AX	K		FAWC	CF	Cwmbran
37431	AX	K		FAWC	CF	County of Powys, Sir Powys

CLASS 37/5   TYPE 3   CO-CO

Built: English Electric 1960-65, refurbished BREL Crewe 1986-88.
Engine: English Electric 12cyl, 4-stroke, 12 CVST of 1,750hp (1,306kW).
Weight: 106-107 tonnes.
Dimensions, Brake force, Maximum tractive effort, Train brakes, Route availability: As Class 37/0.
Power/control equipment, Fuel, Standard equipment: As Class 37/4.

Train heating: Not equipped.
Maximum operating speed: 80mph.
Special characteristics: Slow speed control (s) as shown.

Diagram	Series
37-5AX	First
37-5CX	Second

Sectors:
Railfreight: **FAMT:** Construction, Stone, Tinsley. **FHCC:** Coal, Trainload, Cardiff. **FMYT:** Metals, Thornaby. **FTLL:** China clay, Laira.
Special livery: *British Steel blue:* 37501.

Loc No	Former No	Dia	SC	Liv	Pool	Dep
37501	(37005)	AX		★	FMYT	TE
Teesside Steelmaster						
37502	(37082)	AX		F	FMYT	TE
British Steel Teesside						
37503	(37017)	AX		F	FMYT	TE
British Steel Shelton						
37504	(37039)	AX		F	FMYT	TE
British Steel Corby						
37505	(37028)	AX		F	FMYT	TE
British Steel Workington						
37506	(37007)	AX		F	FMYT	TE
British Steel Skinningrove						
37507	(37036)	AX		Fm	FMYT	TE
BSC Hartlepool Pipe Mill						
37508	(37090)	AX		F	FMYT	TE
37509	(37093)	AX		F	FMYT	TE
37510	(37112)	AX		F	FMYT	TE
37511	(37103)	AX		Fm	FMYT	TE
Stockton Haulage						
37512	(37022)	AX	D	F	FMYT	TE
Thornaby Demon						
37513	(37056)	AX		F	FMYT	TE
37514	(37115)	AX	s	F	FMYT	TE
37515	(37064)	AX	s	F	FMYT	TE
37516	(37086)	AX	s	F	FMYT	TE
37517	(37018)	AX	s	F	FMYT	TE
37518	(37076)	AX		F	FMYT	TE
37519	(37027)	AX		F	FMYT	TE
37520	(37041)	AX		F	FMYT	TE
37521	(37117)	AX		Fm	FMYT	TE

Loc No	Former No	Dia	SC	Liv	Pool	Dep
37667	(37151)	CX	s	Fm	FMYT	TE
Wensleydale						
37668	(37257)	CX	s	Fm	FMYT	TE
Leyburn						
37669	(37129)	CX		F	FTLL	LA
37670	(37182)	CX		F	FTLL	LA
37671	(37247)	CX		F	FTLL	LA
Tre Pol and Pen						
37672	(37189)	CX	s	F	FTLL	LA
Freight Transport Association						
37673	(37132)	CX		Fg	FTLL	LA
37674	(37169)	CX		F	FTLL	LA
37675	(37164)	CX	s	F	FTLL	LA
William Cookworthy						
37676	(37126)	CX		F	FAMT	TI
37677	(37121)	CX		F	FAMT	TI
37678	(37256)	CX		F	FAMT	TI
37679	(37123)	CX		F	FAMT	TI
37680	(37224)	CX		F	FAMT	TI
37681	(37130)	CX		F	FAMT	TI
37682	(37236)	CX		F	FAMT	TI
37683	(37187)	CX		F	FAMT	TI
37684	(37134)	CX		F	FAMT	TI
37685	(37234)	CX		F	FAMT	TI
37686	(37172)	CX		F	FAMT	TI
37687	(37181)	CX		F	FAMT	TI
37688	(37205)	CX		Fa	FAMT	TI
Great Rocks						
37689	(37195)	CX	s	F	FHCC	CF
Coedbach						
37690	(37171)	CX	s	F	FHCC	CF
37691	(37179)	CX	s	F	FHCC	CF

Loc No	Former No	Dia	SC	Liv	Pool	Dep	Loc No	Former No	Dia	SC	Liv	Pool	Dep
37692	(37122)	CX	S		F	FHCC	CF	37696	(37228)	CX	S	F	FHCC	CF
37693	(37210)	CX	S		F	FHCC	CF	37697	(37243)	CX	S	F	FHCC	CF
37694	(37192)	CX			F	FHCC	CF	37698	(37246)	CX	S	F	FHCC	CF
37695	(37157)	CX			F	FHCC	CF	37699	(37253)	CX	S	F	FHCC	CF

CLASS 37/7   TYPE 3   CO-CO

Built: English Electric 1961-65, refurbished and fitted with ballast weights on bogies at BREL Crewe 1986-89.
Engine: English Electric 12cyl, 4-stroke, 12 CVST of 1,750hp (1,306kW).
Dimensions, Brake force, Train brakes, Route availability: As Class 37/0.
Maximum tractive effort: ?
Power/control equipment: Six English Electric traction motors EE538/A; main alternator Brush BA 100 SA or GEC 564 (see below).

Train heating: Not equipped.
Fuel, Maximum operating speed, Standard equipment: As Class 37/5.
Special characteristics: Slow speed control (s).

Diagram	Series	Alternator
37-7AX	First	Brush
37-7BX	First	GEC
37-7CX	Second	Brush
37-7DX	Second	GEC

Sectors:
Railfreight: **FECA:** Coal, Trainload, Aberthaw. **FMCH:** Metals, Steel, Cardiff. **FPLX:** Petroleum, North Thames, Ripple Lane.

Loc No	Former No	Dia	SC	Liv	Pool	Dep	Loc No	Former No	Dia	SC	Liv	Pool	Dep
37701	(37030)	AX	SK	F	FECA	CF	37714	(37024)	AX	K	FM	FMCH	CF
37702	(37020)	AX	SK	F	FECA	CF	37715	(37021)	AX	K	FM	FMCH	CF
37703	(37067)	AX	SK	F	FECA	CF	37716	(37094)	AX		FM	FMCH	CF
37704	(37034)	AX	SK	F	FECA	CF	37718	(37084)	AX		FM	FMCH	CF
37705	(37060)	AX	K	Fp	FPLX	SF	37719	(37033)	AX		FM	FMCH	CF
37706	(37016)	AX	K	Fp	FPLX	SF	37796	(37105)	BX	S	F	FECA	CF
37707	(37001)	AX	K	Fp	FPLX	SF	37797	(37081)	BX	S	F	FECA	CF
37708	(37089)	AX	K	Fp	FPLX	SF	37798	(37006)	BX	S	F	FECA	CF
37709	(37014)	AX	K	Fp	FPLX	SF	37799	(37061)	BX	S	F	FECA	CF
37710	(37044)	AX	K	FM	FMCH	CF		*Sir Dyfed-County of Dyfed*					
37711	(37085)	AX	K	FM	FMCH	CF							
	Tremorfa Steel Works						37800	(37143)	DX	S	F	FECA	CF
								Glo Cymru					
37712	(37102)	AX	K	FM	FMCH	CF							
	Cardiff Rod Mill						37801	(37173)	DX	S	F	FECA	CF
								Aberddawan, Aberthaw					
37713	(37052)	AX	K	FM	FMCH	CF							

Loc No	Former No	Dia	SC	Liv	Pool	Dep	Loc No	Former No	Dia	SC	Liv	Pool	Dep
37802	(37163)	DX	s	F	FECA	CF	37890	(37168)	CX		Fp	FPLX	SF
37803	(37208)	DX	s	F	FECA	CF	37891	(37166)	CX		Fp	FPLX	SF
37883	(37176)	CX		Fm	FMCH	CF	37892	(37149)	CX		Fp	FPLX	SF
37884	(37183)	CX		Fm	FMCH	CF		*Ripple Lane*					
37885	(37177)	CX		Fm	FMCH	CF							
37886	(37180)	CX		Fm	FMCH	CF	37893	(37237)	CX		Fp	FPLX	SF
37887	(37125)	CX	s	Fp	FECA	CF	37894	(37124)	CX	s	F	FECA	CF
37888	(37135)	CX		Fp	FPLX	SF	37895	(37283)	CX	s	F	FECA	CF
	Petrolea						37896	(37231)	CX	s	F	FECA	CF
							37897	(37155)	CX	s	F	FECA	CF
37889	(37233)	CX	s	Fp	FECA	CF	37898	(37186)	CX	s	F	FECA	CF
							37899	(37161)	CX	s	F	FECA	CF

CLASS 37/9   TYPE 3   CO-CO

Built: English Electric 1963/64, rebuilt to present design at BREL Crewe 1986.

Engine: Mirrlees MB275T or GEC Ruston RK270T, 12cyl, 4-stroke of 1,800hp (1,343kN).

Weight: 120 tonnes.

Dimensions: As Class 37/0 Second Series.

Brake force: ?

Maximum tractive effort: ?

Power/control equipment: Six English Electric traction motors EE538/A; main alternator Brush BA100SA or GEC 564.

Train heating: Not equipped.

Train brakes: Dual Air and Vacuum.

Route availability: 7.

Fuel: 1,689gal.

Maximum operating speed: 80mph.

Standard equipment: As Class 37/4.

Special characteristics: Slow speed control (s) as shown.

Diagram	Engine	Alternator
37-9AX	Mirrlees	Brush
37-9BX	GEC	GEC

Sector:

Railfreight: **FMCC:** Metals (Steel), Cardiff.

Loc No	Dia	SC	Liv	Pool	Dep
37901	AX		F	FMCC	CF
	Mirrlees Pioneer				
37902	AX		Fm	FMCC	CF
37903	AX		Fm	FMCC	CF
37904	AX		Fm	FMCC	CF
37905	BX	s	F	FMCC	CF
	Vulcan Enterprise				
37906	BX	s	Fm	FMCC	CF

CLASS 43　　　　　TYPE 4　　　　　BO-BO

INTERCITY 125 POWER CARS

Built: BREL Crewe 1976-82.
Dimensions: 58.4ft L (except Diagram
43-OFA: 59.9ft) ×8.9ft W ×12.8ft H.
Weight: 70 tonnes.
Engine: Paxman Valenta 12cyl, 4-stroke,
12RP200L, V type or Mirrlees Blackstone
12cyl, 4-stroke, MP190, 2,250hp (1,680kW).
Power/control equipment: Four traction
motors Brush THM68-46 or GEC417AZ frame
mounted; main alternator BA1001B.
Train brake: Air.
Locomotive brake: Air.
Brake Force: 50 tonnes.
Maximum operating speed: 125mph.
Maximum tractive effort: 17,900lbs (80kN).
Route availability: 5.
Fuel: 1,000gal.
Standard equipment: Driver/Guard
communication.
Special characteristics: Cab/shore radio (B),
One man operation (M).

Diagram	Type*	Power unit	Traction motors
43-OAA	DMB	Paxman	Brush
43-OBA	DMB	Paxman	GEC
43-OCA	DM	Paxman	Brush
43-ODA	DM	Paxman	GEC
43-OEA	DM	Mirrlees	Brush
43-OFA	DM/TV	Paxman	Brush

*DMB: Driving Motor Brake (Guard's
accommodation retained); DM: Driving
Motor (Guard's accommodation removed);
DM/TV: Driving Motor Trailer Van (Equipped
with TDM Push-Pull equipment and nose-end
buffers).
Train heat: Electric from alternator (for IC125
stock only).

Sectors:
INTERCITY: **ICCP:** Cross Country; **IECP:** East
Coast main line; **IMLP** Midland main line;
IWRP: Western Region main line.
Livery: INTERCITY. Those marked 'I' carry the
latest style with Swallow emblem.

Loc No	Dia	SC	Liv	Pool	Dep
43002	CA		I	IWRP	OO
Top of the Pops					
43003	CA		I	IWRP	OO
43004	CA		I	IWRP	OO
43005	CA		I	IWRP	OO
43006	CA			IWRP	OO
43007	CA			IWRP	OO
43008	CA	B		IWRP	LA
43009	CA			IWRP	LA
43010	CA			IWRP	LA
43011	CA			IWRP	LA
43012	CA		I	ICCP	LA
43013	FA			IECP	BN
University of Bristol					
43014	FA			IECP	BN

Loc No	Dia	SC	Liv	Pool	Dep
43015	CA			IWRP	LA
43016	CA			ICCP	LA
43017	CA			IWRP	LA
HTV West					
43018	AA			IWRP	PM
43019	CA			ICCP	LA
Dinas Abertawe. City of Swansea					
43020	CA			IWRP	LA
43021	AA			IWRP	LA
43022	CA			IWRP	LA
43023	CA			IWRP	LA
43024	CA			IWRP	LA
43025	CA	B		IWRP	LA
43026	CA			IWRP	LA
City of Westminster					

Loc No	Dia	SC	Liv	Pool	Dep
43027	CA			IWRP	LA
	Westminster Abbey				
43028	CA			IWRP	LA
43029	CA			IWRP	LA
43030	CA			IWRP	PM
43031	CA			IWRP	PM
43032	CA			IWRP	PM
43033	CA			IWRP	PM
43034	CA			IWRP	PM
43035	CA		I	ICCP	PM
43036	AA		I	ICCP	PM
43037	CA	B	I	ICCP	PM
43038	CA			IMLP	NL
	National Railway Museum.				
	The First Ten Years 1975-1985				
43039	CA			IMLP	NL
43040	CA	M		IECP	EC
43041	CA	M		IECP	EC
43042	CA			IECP	BN
43043	CA	M		IECP	BN
43044	AA	M		IMLP	NL
43045	CA	M		IMLP	NL
	The Grammar School Doncaster AD 1350				
43046	CA		I	IMLP	NL
43047	CA			IMLP	NL
	Rotherham Enterprise				
43048	CA	B	I	IMLP	NL
43049	CA			IMLP	NL
	Neville Hill				
43050	CA	M		IMLP	NL
43051	CA	M	I	IMLP	NL
	The Duke and Duchess of York				
43052	AA	BM		IECP	NL
	City of Peterborough				
43053	CA			IECP	NL
	County of Humberside				
43054	CA	BM		IECP	NL
43055	CA	M		IMLP	NL
43056	CA	M		IECP	BN
	University of Bradford				
43057	CA	BM		IECP	BN
	Bounds Green				
43058	CA	BM	I	IECP	NL
43059	CA			IECP	NL
43060	CA			IMLP	NL
	County of Leicestershire				
43061	CA	BM	I	IMLP	NL
	City of Lincoln				
43062	CA	M		IECP	BN
43063	CA			IECP	BN
43064	CA			IMLP	NL
	City of York				
43065	FA		I	IMLP	NL
43066	CA	B		IMLP	NL
43067	CA	M	I	IECP	EC
43068	CA	M	I	IECP	EC
43069	CA	M		IECP	EC
43070	CA	M		IECP	EC
43071	CA			IECP	EC
43072	CA		I	IMLP	NL
43073	CA			IMLP	NL
43074	CA			IECP	BN
43075	CA			IECP	BN
43076	CA	M		IMLP	NL
43077	CA	M		IMLP	NL
	County of Nottingham				
43078	CA		I	IECP	EC
	Shildon, County Durham				
43079	CA			IECP	EC
43080	AA			IECP	BN
43081	CA	M		IECP	BN
43082	CA	M		IECP	BN
43083	CA	M		IECP	BN
43084	FA		I	IECP	BN
	County of Derbyshire				
43085	AA			IECP	BN
	City of Bradford				

Loc No	Dia	SC	Liv	Pool	Dep
43086	CA			IECP	EC
43087	CA	M		IECP	EC
43088	CA	M		IECP	EC

XIII Commonwealth Games, Edinburgh 1986

Loc No	Dia	SC	Liv	Pool	Dep
43089	CA			IECP	EC
43090	CA	M	I	IECP	EC
43091	AA			IECP	EC

Edinburgh Military Tattoo

| 43092 | CA | | I | IECP | EC |

Highland Chieftain

| 43093 | CA | | I | IECP | EC |

York Festival '88

| 43094 | CA | | | IECP | EC |
| 43095 | CA | | | IECP | HT |

Heaton

| 43096 | AA | | I | IECP | HT |

The Queen's Own Hussars

| 43097 | CA | M | I | IECP | HT |

The Light Infantry

| 43098 | CA | | I | IECP | HT |

Tyne & Wear Metropolitan County

| 43099 | AA | | | IECP | HT |
| 43100 | AA | M | I | IECP | EC |

Craigentinny

| 43101 | CA | | I | IECP | EC |

Edinburgh International Festival

| 43102 | CA | | I | IECP | HT |

City of Wakefield

| 43103 | CA | | I | IECP | HT |

John Wesley

| 43104 | AA | | I | IECP | HT |

County of Cleveland

| 43105 | CA | | I | IECP | HT |

Hartlepool

Loc No	Dia	SC	Liv	Pool	Dep
43106	AA			IECP	BN
43107	AA	M		IECP	BN

City of Derby

43108	AA			IMLP	NL
43109	AA			IMLP	NL
43110	AA	M		IECP	HT

Darlington

43111	CA		I	IECP	NL
43112	AA	M		IECP	NL
43113	AA	M		IECP	HT

City of Newcastle upon Tyne

43114	AA	M		IECP	BN
43115	AA			IECP	BN
43116	AA	M		IECP	NL

City of Kingston upon Hull

| 43117 | AA | | | IECP | NL |
| 43118 | CA | | I | IECP | NL |

Charles Wesley

43119	AA	M		IECP	NL
43120	CA			IECP	NL
43121	CA			IECP	NL

West Yorkshire Metropolitan County

| 43122 | AA | | | IECP | NL |

South Yorkshire Metropolitan County

| 43123 | FA | | | IECP | BN |
| 43124 | DA | | | IWRP | PM |

BBC Points West

| 43125 | DA | | I | IWRP | PM |

Merchant Venturer

| 43126 | DA | | I | ICCP | PM |

City of Bristol

43127	DA			IWRP	PM
43128	DA		I	IWRP	PM
43129	BA			IWRP	PM
43130	BA			IWRP	PM
43131	DA		I	IWRP	PM

Sir Felix Pole

Loc No	Dia	SC	Liv	Pool	Dep		Loc No	Dia	SC	Liv	Pool	Dep
43132	CA		I	IWRP	PM		43162	CA			IMLP	NL
	Worshipful Company of Carmen							Borough of Stevenage					
43133	DA		I	IWRP	PM		43163	CA		I	ICCP	LA
43134	DA		I	IWRP	PM		43164	CA	B		ICCP	LA
43135	DA		I	IWRP	PM		43165	CA			ICCP	LA
43136	DA		I	IWRP	PM		43166	CA			ICCP	LA
43137	DA			IWRP	PM		43167	EA	B		IWRP	PM
43138	BA			IWRP	PM		43168	EA			IWRP	PM
43139	DA			IWRP	OO		43169	EA	B		IWRP	PM
43140	BA		I	IWRP	OO		43170	EA			IWRP	PM
43141	DA			IWRP	OO		43171	CA		I	ICCP	PM
43142	DA			IWRP	OO		43172	CA			ICCP	PM
	St Mary's Hospital Paddington						43173	CA			ICCP	PM
							43174	CA			ICCP	PM
43143	DA			IWRP	OO		43175	CA			ICCP	PM
43144	DA			IWRP	OO		43176	CA			IWRP	PM
43145	BA		I	IWRP	OO		43177	CA			ICCP	LA
43146	DA		I	IWRP	OO		43178	CA		I	ICCP	LA
43147	BA		I	IWRP	OO		43179	CA			ICCP	LA
43148	BA		I	IWRP	OO		43180	CA			IWRP	OO
43149	BA		I	IWRP	PM		43181	CA			ICCP	LA
	BBC Wales Today						43182	CA			ICCP	LA
							43183	CA			ICCP	LA
43150	BA		I	IWRP	PM		43184	CA			ICCP	LA
	Bristol Evening Post						43185	CA		I	ICCP	LA
							43186	CA		I	ICCP	LA
43151	DA			IWRP	PM		43187	CA			IWRP	LA
	Blue Peter II						43188	CA			IWRP	LA
								City of Plymouth					
43152	DA			IMLP	NL								
	St Peter's School York AD 627						43189	CA		I	IWRP	LA
							43190	CA		I	IWRP	LA
43153	CA			IMLP	NL		43191	CA			IWRP	LA
	University of Durham						43192	CA			IWRP	LA
							43193	CA			IMLP	NL
43154	CA			IECP	NL			Yorkshire Post					
43155	CA			IECP	NL								
	BBC Look North						43194	CA		I	IECP	NL
								Royal Signals					
43156	CA			IECP	NL								
43157	CA			IECP	NL		43195	CA			IECP	NL
	Yorkshire Evening Post						43196	CA			IECP	NL
								The Newspaper Society					
43158	CA			IMLP	NL								
43159	CA			IECP	NL		43197	CA			IECP	NL
43160	CA			IECP	NL		43198	CA			IECP	NL
43161	CA			IMLP	NL								

CLASS 45/1   TYPE 4   1CO-CO1

Built: British Rail 1961.
Engine: Sulzer 12cyl 12LDA28-B of 2,500hp (1,865kW).
Weight: 135 tonnes.
Dimensions: 67.9ft L × 9.1ft W × 12.8ft H.
Brake force: 63 tonnes.
Maximum tractive effort: 55,000lb.
Power/control equipment: Six Crompton Parkinson C172A1 traction motors; main generator Crompton Parkinson CG426A1.

Route availability: 6.
Fuel: 790gal.
Train brake: Dual Air and Vacuum.
Maximum operating speed: 90mph.
Diagram: 45-1AX.
Standard equipment: Sanding gear, Headlight (L).
Train heating: Electric alternator, Brush BL100-30 Mk II driven by main engine.
ETH Index: 66

Sector:
InterCity: **ICHA:** Charter.
Special livery: *Green:* 45106.

Loc No	Dia	SC	Liv	Pool	Dep
45106	AX			ICHA	TI

CLASS 47/0   TYPE 4   CO-CO

Built: British Railways and Brush Engineering Ltd 1962-67.
Engine: Sulzer 12cyl, 4-stroke, 12LDA28C of 2,580hp (1,925kW).
Power/control equipment: see below.
Weight: see below.
Dimensions: 63.6ft L × 9.2ft W × 12.8ft H.
Brake force: 60 tonnes.
Maximum tractive effort: 62,000lb (267kN).
Route availability: 6.
Train brake: Dual Air and Vacuum.
Maximum operating speed: 75mph (originally 95mph).

Train heating: (see also below): Steam generator, where fitted, isolated. *Types:* **B:** Clayton Mk II, 2,500lb/hr; **C:** Stone Vapor 4625, 2,750lb/hr; **D:** Spanner Swirlyflow Mk III, 1,850lb/hr; **O:** Not fitted. Boiler water (see below)*: Water tanks have not been retained by all locomotives, but this data is not available from published DMEE specifications.
Standard equipment: Headlights (L); One man operation (M).
Special characteristics: Cab-shore radio (B); Snowplough brackets (K); Extra 250gal fuel tank (X).

Diagram	Weight tonnes	Main Generator Brush	Traction Motors Six Brush	Fuel (gal)	Train Heat/ Boiler Water
47-0BX	120.6	TG160-60 Mk 2	TM64-68 Mk 1	720	D.1,250gal
47-0EX	120.4	TG160-60 Mk 4	TM64-68 Mk 1	720	D.1,200gal
47-0GX	119.1	TG172-50 Mk 1	TM64-68 Mk 1A	720	C.1,200gal
47-0HX	118.8	TG172-50 Mk 1	TM64-68 Mk 1A	720	B.1,200gal
47-0LX	111.5	TG172-50 Mk 1	TM64-68 Mk 1A	720	O.1,200gal*
47-0MX	119.3	TG160-60 Mk 2	TM64-68 Mk 1	720	O.1,250gal*
47-0NX	118.8	TG172-50 Mk 1	TM64-68 Mk 1A	970	O.1,200gal*

Sectors:
Departmental: **DCHA:** DCE Scotland. **DCMA:** DCE Midland.
Railfreight: **FAME:** Construction (Stone), Eastfield. **FAWC:** Construction (Stone) Cardiff Canton.
  FGWA: Distribution (Speedlink). **FPLC:** Petroleum, Stanlow. **FPLI:** Petroleum, Immingham.
  FPLW: Petroleum, South Wales. **FTLC:** Chemicals, Crewe.
Freightliner: **LNRB:** Anglia, Stratford. **LNRC:** General, Crewe.

Loc No	Dia	SC	Liv	Pool	Dep
47002	MX	B		FGWA	TI
47003	BX	BK		DCMA	ED
47004	BX	BK		FAME	ED
47005	MX	B		FGWA	TI
47006	MX	BK		FAME	ED
47007	MX			LNRB	SF
Stratford					
47008	BX			LNRC	CD
47009	BX	B		LNRC	CD
47010	MX	B		FPLC	CD
47012	BX			FGWA	TI
47014	MX			LNRB	SF
47016	MX			FGWA	TI
The Toleman Group					
47017	DX	BK		FAME	ED
47018	MX	K		DCMA	ED
47019	MX			LNRC	CD
47033	LX	B		FAWC	CF
47049	GX			FGWA	TI
47050	LX			FTLC	CD
47051	LX			LNRC	CD
47052	LX			FGWA	TI
47053	GX	K		DCMA	ED
47054	HX			FPLI	IM
47060	HX		FG	FGWA	TI
Halewood Silver Jubilee 1988					

Loc No	Dia	SC	Liv	Pool	Dep
47063	LX	B		FAWC	CF
47079	LX	B	FM	FAWC	CF
47085	HX	B	FP	FPLC	CD
Conidae					
47094	LX			FPLW	CF
47095	LX			FGWA	TI
47096	BX			LNRB	SF
47097	MX			FGWA	TI
47098	MX	B		FGWA	TI
47099	MX			LNRB	SF
47100	MX			LNRB	SF
47101	BX	B		LNRC	CD
47102	BX			FGWA	TI
47105	BX			LNRB	SF
47107	LX			FGWA	TI
47108	BX	B		LNRB	SF
47110	MX	B		FGWA	TI
47112	MX			LNRB	SF
47114	EX	B		FALG	SF
47115	BX			FGWA	TI
47116	BX			LNRB	SF
47117	BX	BK		FGWA	TI
47118	BX	K		DCMA	ED
47119	MX		FP	FPLC	CD
Arcidae					
47120	BX			FGWA	TI
RAF Kinloss					

Loc No	Dia	SC	Liv	Pool	Dep
47121	BX	B		LNRB	SF
47123	BX			LNRB	SF
47124	BX			LNRC	CD
47125	LX		Fp	FPLC	CD
Tonnidae					
47142	LX	B	F	FGWA	TI
The Sapper					
47143	LX	B		FGWA	TI
47144	EX			FGWA	TI
47146	EX	B		FGWA	TI
47147	LX	B		FGWA	TI
47150	EX	B		FGWA	TI
47152	EX	B		FGWA	TI
47156	EX			FGWA	TI
47157	LX		F	FGWA	TI
47186	LX		F	FMCA	CF
47187	GX	B		FMCA	CF
47188	LX			FGWA	TI
47190	LX		Fp	FPLC	CD
Pectinidae					
47193	LX		Fp	FPLC	CD
Lucinidae					
47194	GX		Fp	FPLC	CD
Bullidae					
47195	GX	B	Fp	FPLC	CD
Muricidae					
47196	LX		Fp	FPLC	CD
Haliotidae					
47197	GX			FPLW	CF
47198	LX	B		FPLW	CF
47200	GX	B		FGWA	TI
47201	GX	B		FGWA	TI
47203	GX			FGWA	TI
47204	LX			FGWA	TI
47205	GX			FGWA	TI
47206	GX	K		FGWA	TI
47207	LX	B	Fg	FGWA	TI
Bulmers of Hereford					
47209	GX			FGWA	TI

Loc No	Dia	SC	Liv	Pool	Dep
47210	GX	BK		FAME	ED
47211	LX	B	F	FGWA	TI
47212	NX	XB		FPLI	IM
47213	LX	B	F	FGWA	TI
47214	LX			FGWA	TI
Tinsley Traction Depot					
47215	LX		F	FGWA	TI
47217	GX			FGWA	TI
47218	LX			FGWA	TI
47219	GX	B		FGWA	TI
47220	LX		F	FGWA	TI
47221	LX			FPLC	IM
47222	LX	B		FPLI	IM
Appleby Frodingham					
47223	GX	B		FPLI	IM
47224	LX	B		FPLI	IM
47225	LX	B		FGWA	TI
47226	LX			FGWA	TI
47227	LX	B	F	FTLC	CD
47228	HX			FTLC	CD
47229	LX	B		FTLC	CD
47231	LX		Fg	FGWA	TI
The Silcock Express					
47233	LX		Fp	FPLC	CD
Strombidae					
47234	LX			FGWA	TI
47235	LX		F	FGWA	TI
47236	LX		F	FGWA	TI
47237	LX		F	FGWA	TI
47238	LX			FGWA	TI
Bescot Yard					
47241	LX			FGWA	TI
47245	LX			FGWA	TI
47249	LX		F	FGWA	TI
47256	LX	B		FGWA	SF
47258	LX	B		FGWA	TI
47270	LX	B		FGWA	TI
47276	NX	XB		FPLI	IM
47277	LX	B		FPLI	IM
47278	LX	P	Fp	FPLC	CD
47279	HX	B	Fg	FGWA	TI
47280	LX		F	FGWA	TI
Pedigree					

43

Loc No	Dia	SC	Liv	Pool	Dep		Loc No	Dia	SC	Liv	Pool	Dep
47281	LX	B		FMCA	CF		47291	LX		F	LNRB	SF
47283	LX		FG	FGWA	TI			The Port of Felixstowe				
	Johnnie Walker											
							47292	LX			FGWA	TI
47284	LX			FGWA	TI		47293	LX	B		FGWA	TI
47285	LX		F	FGWA	TI		47294	LX	B		FPLC	IM
47286	LX	B		FGWA	TI		47295	NX	XB		FPLI	IM
47287	LX			FGWA	TI		47296	LX			FGWA	TI
47288	LX			FGWA	TI		47297	LX			FGWA	TI
47289	LX			FGWA	TI		47298	HX			FGWA	TI
47290	HX		F	FGWA	TI		47299	NX	XB		FPLI	IM

CLASS 47/3   TYPE 4   CO-CO

Built: Brush Engineering Ltd 1964/65.
Engine, Dimensions, Maximum tractive effort, Brake force, Route availability, Train brakes: As Class 47/0.
Power/control equipment: Six Brush TM64-68 Mk 1A traction motors; main generator TG172-50 Mk 1.
Train heat, Boiler water: Not equipped.

Diagram	Fuel (gal)
47-3AX	720
47-3BX	970

Standard equipment: Headlights (L); One man operation (M); Slow speed control (S); Sanding gear.
Special characteristics: Cab-shore radio (B).

Sectors:
Departmental: **DCAA:** DCE Anglia Region. **DCEA:** DCE Eastern Region. **DCMA:** DCE Midland Region.
Railfreight: **FALG:** Construction, (Stone) Stratford. **FAWC:** Construction (Stone), Cardiff Canton. **FGWA:** Distribution (Speedlink). **FMCA:** Metals (Steel), Cardiff Canton. **FMYT:** Metals (Steel), Thornaby. **FPLI:** Petroleum, Immingham. **FPLW:** Petroleum, South Wales. **FTLC:** Chemicals, Crewe.
Freightliner: **LNRC:** General, Crewe.

Loc No	Dia	SC	Liv	Pool	Dep		Loc No	Dia	SC	Liv	Pool	Dep
47301	AX			FTYT	TE		47311	AX		FG	FGWA	TI
47302	AX	B		FTYT	TE			Warrington Yard				
47303	AX	B	Fx	FTYT	TE							
47304	AX	B		FTYT	TE		47312	AX			FGWA	TI
47305	AX	B	FP	FTYT	TE		47313	AX	B		FGWA	TI
47306	AX			FGWA	TI		47314	AX			FGWA	TI
47307	AX			FGWA	TI		47315	AX			FGWA	TI
47308	AX		F-	FGWA	TI		47316	AX	B		FGWA	TI
47309	AX			FGWA	TI		47317	AX	B	FG	FGWA	TI
47310	AX	B		FGWA	TI			Willesden Yard				

Loc No	Dia	SC	Liv	Pool	Dep
47318	AX	B	F	FPLW	CF
47319	AX		FG	FPLI	IM
Norsk Hydro					
47320	AX		F	FALG	SF
47321	AX			FGWA	TI
47322	AX			FTLC	CD
47323	AX	B		FTLC	CD
47324	AX	B	FP	FPLC	CD
Glossidae					
47325	AX	B	F	FTLC	SF
47326	AX			FPLW	CF
47327	AX	B	F	FPLW	CF
47328	AX	B		FALG	SF
47329	AX	B		DCEA	IM
47330	AX	B		LNRC	CD
47331	AX	B	F	DCEA	IM
47332	AX	B		DCEA	IM
47333	AX	B		DCMA	OC
47334	AX	B		FPLW	CF
47335	AX	B		LNRC	CD
47336	AX			FPLI	IM
47337	AX		F	FGWA	TI
Herbert Austin					
47338	AX	B		FGWA	TI
47339	AX	B		DCMA	CD
47340	AX			DCMA	CD
47341	AX	B		DWCA	OC
47342	AX			LNRC	CD
47343	AX	B		DCMA	CD
47344	AX			DCEA	IM
47345	AX	B		LNRC	CD
47346	AX		F	DCAA	SF
47347	AX			FMYT	TE
47348	AX	B	F	DCEA	IM
St Christopher's Railway Home					
47349	AX	B		LNRC	CD
47350	AX	B	F	LNRC	CD
British Petroleum					
47351	AX	B		LNRC	CD
47352	AX	B		DCEA	IM
47353	AX			DCMA	CD
47354	AX	B		LNRC	CD
47355	AX			LNRC	CD
47356	AX	B	F	DCMA	CD
47357	AX			DCMA	CD
47358	AX		F	DCMA	CD
47359	AX	B	FM	FMCA	CF
47360	AX			FGWA	TI
47361	AX	B		FTYT	TE
Wilton Endeavour					
47362	AX	B	F	FTYT	TE
47363	AX	B	F	FTYT	TE
Billingham Enterprise					
47364	AX	B		LNRC	CD
47365	AX	B	F	FTLC	CD
Diamond Jubilee					
47366	AX	B	F	DCAA	SF
The Institution of Civil Engineers					
47367	AX		F	FALG	SF
47368	AX	B	F	FPLC	CD
Neritidae					
47369	AX			FPLW	CF
47370	AX		F	FGWA	TI
47371	AX		F	FGWA	TI
47372	AX			FGWA	TI
47373	AX		F	FPLI	IM
47374	AX	B	F	FPLI	IM
47375	AX	B		FGWA	TI
47376	AX			FGWA	TI
47377	AX	B		FGWA	TI
47378	AX	B	F	FGWA	TI
47379	AX	B	F	FPLI	IM
Total Energy					
47380	BX	XB	FP	FPLI	IM
Immingham					
47381	AX		F-	FPLW	CF

45

CLASS 47/4   TYPE 4   CO-CO

Built: British Railways and Brush Engineering Ltd 1962-67.
Engine, Dimensions, Brake force, Train brake: As Class 47/0.
Route availability: 7
Power/control equipment: see below.
Weight and Fuel: see below.
Maximum operating speed: 95mph (except SC '75' see below).
Train heating: (see also below): *Electric types:* **H&K:** Brush Electric Generator TG160-16; **E, M** and **N:** Brush Alternator BL100-30. (see SC 'u')

Steam generator types: where fitted, isolated. **E** and **H:** not fitted. **K:** Spanner Swirlyflow Mk IV, 2,500lb/hr. **M:** Spanner Swirlyflow Mk III, 1,850lb/hr. **N:** Stone Vapor 4,625, 2,750lb/hr.
Boiler water: see Class 47/0.
ETH Index: 66. (400amps, except § (see below), 600amps).
Standard equipment: Headlights (L); One man operation (M).
Special characteristics: Cab-shore radio (B); Snowplough brackets (K); Phosphor brake blocks, maximum speed 75mph (75); Electric alternator isolated (U).

Diagram	Weight tonnes	Traction Motors Brush	Main Generator Brush	Fuel (gal)	Train Heat/ Boiler Water
47-4AX	121.4	TM64-68 Mk 1	TG160-60	720	K.1,250gal
47-4BX	122.6	TM64-68 Mk 1	TG160-60 Mk 2	720	M.1,250gal
47-4CX	120.4	TM64-68 Mk 1	TG160-60 Mk 2	720	E.1,250gal*
47-4DX	121.9	TM64-68 Mk 1A	TG160-60 Mk 4	720	M.1,250gal
47-4EX	121.0	TM64-68 Mk 1A	TG160-60 Mk 4	720	E.1,250gal*
47-4FX	123.6	TM64-68 Mk 1A	TG172-50 Mk 1	720	M.1,250gal
47-4GX	125.1	TM64-68 Mk 1A	TG172-50 Mk 1	720	N.1,200gal
47-4HX	122.6	TM64-68 Mk 1A	TG172-50 Mk 1	720	E.1,200gal
47-4JX	123.4	TM64-68 Mk 1A	TG172-50 Mk 1	720	M.1,200gal
47-4KX§	122.6	TM64-68 Mk 1A	TG172-50 Mk 1	720	E.1,200gal
47-4LX	120.4	TM64-68 Mk 1	TG160-60	720	H.—*
47-4MX§	122.6	TM64-68 Mk 1A	TG172-50 Mk 1	1,295	E.—

Note: Locomotives to Diagram 47-4MX may be reclassified 47/8, and renumbered from 47850.
Sectors:
Departmental: **DCHA:** DCE Scottish Region. **DCWA:** DCE, Western Region.
Railfreight: **FGWA:** Distribution (Speedlink). **FMYT:** Metals, Thornaby. **FTLC:** Chemicals, Crewe.
InterCity: **ICCA:** Cross Country. **ICHA:** Charter. **IWCA:** West Coast main line. **IWRA:** Western Region.
Network SouthEast: **NNEA:** Northeast. **NSSA:** Solent and Sarum. **NWRA:** Western Region.
Provincial: **PTPA:** Trans-Pennine, North. **PXXA:** General.
Parcels: **RXLD:** General.
Special liveries: *GWR Brunswick Green:* 47484, 47500, 47628.
LNER Apple Green: 47522.

Loc No	Dia	SC	Liv	Pool	Dep	Loc No	Dia	SC	Liv	Pool	Dep
47401	LX			RXLD	IM	47450	EX			DCMA	CD
47402	AX	B		RXLD	IM	47451	EX			LNRC	CD
47406	AX			PCRA	IM	47452	EX			LNRB	SF
47407	LX	B		PCRA	IM	47453	EX	B		DCMA	CD
47411	AX			FGXX	IM	47454	EX	B		FTLC	CD
47413	LX			PCRA	IM	47455	HX			RXLD	SF
47417	AX			DCEA	IM	47456	HX			FTLC	CD
47418	AX	B		DCEA	IM	47457	FX			LNRC	CD
47421	BX	75		FGWA	TI						

Ben Line

Loc No	Dia	SC	Liv	Pool	Dep	Loc No	Dia	SC	Liv	Pool	Dep
47422	BX			PTPA	CD	47458	HX	B		RXLD	SF
47423	BX	B		FTLC	CD	47459	HX			IWCA	CD
47424	CX	B		PTPA	CD	47460	FX	BK		PXXA	IS
						47461	HX	BK	Ps	PXXA	IS

The Brontes of Haworth

Charles Rennie Mackintosh

Loc No	Dia	SC	Liv	Pool	Dep	Loc No	Dia	SC	Liv	Pool	Dep
47425	BX			FTLC	CD	47462	HX	B		LNRB	SF

Holbeck

Loc No	Dia	SC	Liv	Pool	Dep	Loc No	Dia	SC	Liv	Pool	Dep
47426	BX			DCMA	CD	47463	HX	B		DCWA	CD
47427	CX	B		DCMA	CD	47465	HX	B		RXLD	SF
47428	CX			DCMA	CD	47466	HX	B		RXLD	BR
47430	BX	B	Is	LNRB	SF	47467	HX	BK		DCHA	IS
47431	CX			DCMA	CD	47468	HX			RXLD	BR
47432	CX			DCMA	CD	47469	HX	BK	Is	PXXA	IS
47433	CX	75		FGWA	TI						

Glasgow Chamber of Commerce

Loc No	Dia	SC	Liv	Pool	Dep	Loc No	Dia	SC	Liv	Pool	Dep
47434	CX	B		PTPA	CD	47470	HX	BK		ICCA	ED
47435	DX	B		RXLD	SF						

University of Edinburgh

Loc No	Dia	SC	Liv	Pool	Dep	Loc No	Dia	SC	Liv	Pool	Dep
47436	EX	B		DCMA	CD	47471	HX	B	I	IECA	CD
47438	EX	B		DCMA	CD						

Norman Tunna G.C.

Loc No	Dia	SC	Liv	Pool	Dep	Loc No	Dia	SC	Liv	Pool	Dep
47439	EX	B		FTLC	CD	47473	HX			NSSA	LA
47440	EX			FTLC	CD	47474	HX	75		FGWA	TI
47441	EX			FTLC	CD	47475	HX			PTPA	CD
47442	EX	B		FTLC	CD	47476	HX	B		RXLD	BR
47443	EX			PTPA	CD	47477	HX			RXLD	BR
47444	EX	B		PTPA	CD	47478	HX			ICCA	CD

University of Nottingham

Loc No	Dia	SC	Liv	Pool	Dep	Loc No	Dia	SC	Liv	Pool	Dep
47445	EX			FTLC	CD	47479	HX			LNRC	CD
47446	EX	B		FTLC	CD	47481	HX	B		LNRC	OC
47447	EX	B		FTLC	CD	47482	HX	B		RXLD	SF
47448	EX	B		PTPA	CD	47483	HX	B		IWCA	CD
47449	EX	B		FTLC	CD						

Loc No	Dia	SC	Liv	Pool	Dep
47484	HX	B	★	DWCC	OC
Isambard Kingdom Brunel					
47485	CX	B		FTLC	CD
47487	CX		I	FTLC	CD
47488	CX			PTPA	CD
Rail Riders					
47489	HX			RXLD	BR
47490	HX	B	I	RXLD	BR
47491	HX			FTLC	CD
Horwich Enterprise					
47492	HX	BK	Is	PXXA	IS
The Enterprising Scot					
47500	HX		★	ICHA	BR
Great Western					
47501	HX	B	I	RXLD	BR
Craftsman					
47503	HX			PTPA	CD
47508	HX		I	ICHA	BR
S.S. Great Britain					
47509	HX	B	I	ICHA	CD
Albion					
47512	HX	B		ICCA	CD
47513	HX			DWCA	OC
Severn					
47515	HX		I	RXLD	ED
Night Mail					
47517	KX	B		IWCA	CD
Andrew Carnegie					
47518	HX			DCHA	ED
47519	HX			ICCA	BR
47520	GX	B		ICCA	CD
47521	GX	B		ICCA	CD
47522	HX			RXLD	SF
Doncaster Enterprise					
47523	GX			RXLD	SF

Loc No	Dia	SC	Liv	Pool	Dep
47524	GX	B		RXLD	ED
47525	HX	B	I	ICCA	BR
47526	HX			RXLD	BR
Northumbria					
47527	GX	B		ICCA	CD
47528	GX	B		RXLD	BR
47530	HX			IWCA	CD
47531	HX	B		FTLC	CD
47532	HX	B		FTLC	CD
47533	HX			RXLD	BR
47534	HX	B		RXLD	BR
47535	HX			RXLD	BR
University of Leicester					
47536	HX			RXLD	BR
47537	HX	B		RXLD	BR
Sir Gwynedd. County of Gwynedd					
47538	HX			RXLD	BR
47539	HX	B		RXLD	BR
Rochdale Pioneers					
47540	HX			DCWA	OC
47541	HX	BK	Is	PXXA	IS
The Queen Mother					
47542	JX			RXLD	BR
47543	HX			RXLD	BR
47544	JX			IWCA	CD
47546	HX	BK		DCHA	IS
Aviemore Centre					
47547	HX			NSSA	LA
47549	HX	B	I	RXLD	ED
Royal Mail					
47550	HX	BK		DCHA	IS
University of Dundee					
47551	MX	XB		ICCA	BR
47552	MX	XB		ICCA	BR
47553	MX	XB	I	IWCA	CD
47555	HX	B	I	ICHA	CD
The Commonwealth Spirit					
47556	KX			ICCA	BR

48

Loc No	Dia	SC	Liv	Pool	Dep
47557	KX	B		RXLD	BR
47558	KX			RXLD	BR
Mayflower					
47559	KX	B		RXLD	BR
Sir Joshua Reynolds					
47560	KX	B	I	IWRA	BR
Tamar					
47562	KX	BK		IWCA	ED
Sir William Burrell					
47563	KX	B		PXXA	IS
Womens' Guild					
47564	KX	B		RXLD	BR
Colossus					
47565	KX			RXLD	BR
47566	KX			RXLD	BR
47567	KX			RXLD	BR
Red Star					
47568	KX			RXLD	BR
47569	KX	B		RXLD	ED
47570	KX	B		IWCA	ED
47571	KX			ICCA	CD
47572	KX	B		RXLD	SF
Ely Cathedral					
47573	KX		N	NWRA	OC
The London Standard					
47574	KX			RXLD	SF
Benjamin Gimbert G.C.					
47575	KX			RXLD	BR
City of Hereford					
47576	KX		N	NNEA	SF
King's Lynn					
47577	KX	B		IECA	CD
47578	KX	BK		PXXA	IS
Royal Society of Edinburgh					
47579	KX		N	NNEA	SF
James Nightall G.C.					
47580	KX			RXLD	SF
County of Essex					
47581	KX		N	NNEA	SF
Great Eastern					
47582	KX		N	NWRA	OC
County of Norfolk					
47583	KX		N	NWRA	OC
County of Hertfordshire					
47584	KX			RXLD	BR
County of Suffolk					
47585	KX			RXLD	SF
County of Cambridgeshire					
47586	KX	B		IMLA	CD
47587	KX			NSSA	LA
47588	KX	B	Fg	FGWA	TI
47589	KX		I	ICCA	CD
47590	KX			RXLD	BR
Thomas Telford					
47591	MX	XB		ICCA	BR
47592	KX			RXLD	BR
County of Avon					
47593	KX	BK	I	ICCA	ED
Galloway Princess					
47594	KX	B		FMYT	TE
47595	KX	BK		IWCA	ED
Confederation of British Industry					
47596	KX	B,75		FGWA	TI
Aldeburgh Festival					
47597	KX	B		IWCA	ED
47598	KX			NSSA	SF
47599	KX	B,75	Fm	FGWA	TI
47600	KX	B,75	Fg	FGWA	TI
Dewi Sant. Saint David					

Loc No	Dia	SC	Liv	Pool	Dep
47602	KX		I	ICCA	CD
Glorious Devon					
47603	KX			RXLD	BR
County of Somerset					
47604	KX	BK		DCHA	ED
Women's Royal Voluntary Service					
47605	KX	B		FTLC	CD
47606	KX		I	ICCA	CD
Odin					
47607	KX	B,75	I	ICCA	CD
Royal Worcester					
47608	KX			ICCA	CD
47609	KX	B	I	ICHA	BR
Fire Fly					
47610	KX	B		ICCA	CD
47611	KX		I	IWRA	BR
Thames					
47612	KX		I	ICCA	CD
Titan					
47613	KX		I	IWRA	BR
North Star					
47614	KX	B		IWCA	ED
47615	KX	75	Fg	FGWA	TI
Castell Caerffili. Caerphilly Castle					
47616	KX	B		RXLD	BR
Y Ddraig Goch. The Red Dragon					
47617	KX	BK		DCHA	IS
University of Stirling					
47618	KX	B	I	IWCA	CD
Fair Rosamund					
47619	KX			IWCA	CD
47620	KX	B	I	ICHA	BR
Windsor Castle					
47621	KX		I	IWRA	BR
Royal County of Berkshire					
47622	KX	B	I	ICCA	ED
The Institution of Mechanical Engineers					
47623	KX			DCWA	OC
Vulcan					
47624	KX			RXLD	BR
Cyclops					
47625	KX	B		RXLD	BR
47626	KX	B		RXLD	BR
Atlas					
47627	KX	B		RXLD	BR
City of Oxford					
47628	KX		★	DCWA	OC
Sir Daniel Gooch					
47629	KX	B		IWCA	BR
47630	KX	BK		PXXA	IS
47631	KX	B		RXLD	BR
47632	KX	B		IWCA	ED
47633	KX	B		ICCA	ED
Orion					
47634	KX			RXLD	BR
Henry Ford					
47635	KX	B		PXXA	IS
Jimmy Milne					
47636	KX	BK		ICCA	ED
Sir John de Graeme					
47637	KX		Is	IWCA	CD
47638	KX	B		IWCA	CD
County of Kent					
47639	KX			IWCA	CD
Industry Year 1986					
47640	KX	B		PXXA	IS
University of Strathclyde					

Loc No	Dia	SC	Liv	Pool	Dep
47641	KX	BK		PXXA	IS
Fife Region					
47642	KX	B	Is	PXXA	IS
Strathisla					
47643	KX	BK	Is	PXXA	IS
47644	KX	BK		PXXA	IS
The Permanent Way Institution					
47645	KX	B		IWCA	CD
Robert F. Fairlie					
47646	KX			IWCA	CD
47647	KX			IWCA	CD
Thor					
47648	KX			IWCA	CD
47649	KX	B		IWCA	ED

Loc No	Dia	SC	Liv	Pool	Dep
47650	MX	XB		ICCA	BR
47651	MX	XB		ICCA	BR
47652	MX	X		ICCA	BR
47653	MX	X		ICCA	BR
47654	MX	X		ICCA	BR
Finsbury Park					
47655	MX	X		ICCA	BR
47656	MX	X		ICCA	BR
47657	MX	XB		ICCA	BR
47658	MX	X		ICCA	BR
47659	MX	XB		ICCA	BR
47660	MX	X		ICCA	BR
47661	MX	X		ICHA	BR
47662	MX	X		ICHA	BR
47663	MX	X		ICHA	BR
47664	MX	X		ICCA	BR
47665	MX	X		ICCA	BR

CLASS 47/7   TYPE 4   CO-CO

Built: British Railways and Brush Engineering Ltd 1966-67. Modified to this specification by BREL from 1979.
Weight: 118.7 tonnes.
Engine, Dimensions, Brake force, Maximum tractive effort, Train brake: As Class 47/0.
Route availability: 7
Power/control equipment: Six Brush Traction Motors TM64-68 Mk 1A; main generator Brush TG172-50 Mk 1.

Fuel: 1,295gal.
Maximum operating speed: 100mph.
Train heating: Brush Electric alternator BL100-30.
ETH Index: 66.
Diagram: 47-7AX
Standard equipment: Cab/shore radio (B); Headlights (L); One man operation (M); Push-Pull operation (P).

Sectors:
Provincial: **PXXA:** General.
Livery: *Provincial ScotRail.*

Loc No	Dia	SC	Liv	Pool	Dep	Name
47701	AX			PXXA	ED	*Saint Andrew*
47702	AX			PXXA	ED	*Saint Cuthbert*

Loc No	Dia	SC	Liv	Pool	Dep	Name
47703	AX			PXXA	ED	Saint Mungo
47704	AX			PXXA	ED	Dunedin
47705	AX			PXXA	ED	Lothian
47706	AX			PXXA	ED	
47707	AX			PXXA	ED	Holyrood
47708	AX			PXXA	ED	Waverley
47709	AX			PXXA	ED	The Lord Provost
47710	AX			PXXA	ED	Sir Walter Scott
47711	AX			PXXA	ED	Greyfriars Bobby
47712	AX			PXXA	ED	Lady Diana Spencer
47714	AX			PXXA	ED	Grampian Region
47715	AX			PXXA	ED	Haymarket
47716	AX			PXXA	ED	The Duke of Edinburgh's Award
47717	AX			PXXA	ED	Tayside Region

Note: No 47717 was converted by BRML Doncaster from No 47497 during 1988 using some equipment from withdrawn locomotive, fire damaged No 47713.

CLASS 47/9   TYPE 5   CO-CO

Built: British Railways 1964. Modified to this design at BREL Crewe in 1979.
Engine: Ruston-Paxman 12cyl, 4-stroke, 12RK3CT of 3,250hp (2,460kW).
Power/control equipment: Six Brush Traction Motors TM64-68 Mk 1A; main generator Brush BA1101.
Weight: 113.7 tonnes.
Dimensions, Brake force: As Class 47/0.
Maximum tractive effort: 57,325lb (516kN).

Route availability: 6.
Fuel: 1,610gal.
Train brake: Air.
Maximum operating speed: 75mph.
Train heating: Not equipped.
Diagram: 47-9AA.
Standard equipment: Cab/shore radio (B); One man operation (M); Slow speed control (S).

Sector:
Railfreight: **FAWC:** Construction (Stone), Cardiff.
Livery: **Railfreight Construction.** (FA).

Loc No	Dia	SC	Liv	Pool	Dep
47901	AA		FA	FAWC	CF

52

CLASS 50/0　　　　TYPE 4　　　　CO-CO

Built: English Electric 1967-68.
Engine: English Electric 16cyl, 4-stroke, 16CSVT of 2,700hp (2,014kW).
Weight: 116.9 tonnes.
Dimensions: 68.5ft L × 9.1ft W × 12.8ft H.
Power/control equipment: Six English Electric traction Motors EE538/5A, main generator EE840/4B.
Train brake: Dual Air and Vacuum.
Brake force: 59 tonnes.
Maximum tractive effort: 48,500lb (216kN).

Fuel: 1,055gal.
Maximum operating speed: 100mph.
Train heating: Electric generator, English Electric EE915/1B.
ETH Index: 61.
Diagram: 50-0AX.
Standard equipment: Snowplough brackets (κ), Headlights (ʟ), One man operationa (м), Multiple Working (Orange Square, code 2).
Special characteristics: Cab-shore Radio (в).

Sectors:
Departmental: **DCWA:** DCE Western Region.
Network SouthEast: **NSSA:** Solent and Sarum. **NWRA:** Western Region (Thames & Chiltern).
Parcels: **RXXA:** General.
Special livery: *GWR Brunswick Green:* 50007.

Loc No	Dia	SC	Liv	Pool	Dep	Name
50001	AX	в	N	NSSA	LA	Dreadnought
50002	AX	в	N	NSSA	LA	Superb
50003	AX	в	N	NSSA	LA	Temeraire
50004	AX			DCWA	LA	St Vincent
50005	AX	в	N	DCWA	LA	Collingwood
50007	AX	в		DCWA	LA	Sir Edward Elgar
50008	AX			DCWA	LA	Thunderer
50009	AX			DCWA	LA	Conqueror
50012	AX			DCWA	LA	Benbow
50015	AX			DCWA	LA	Valiant
50016	AX			DCWA	LA	Barham
50017	AX	в	N	NSSA	LA	Royal Oak
50018	AX		N	NSSA	LA	Resolution
50019	AX	в	N	NSSA	LA	Ramillies
50020	AX			DCWA	LA	Revenge
50021	AX			DCWA	LA	Rodney
50023	AX		N	NWRA	OC	Howe
50024	AX	в	N	NWRA	OC	Vanguard
50025	AX	в	N	NWRA	OC	Invincible
50026	AX	в	N	NWRA	OC	Indomitable
50027	AX	в	N	NSSA	LA	Lion
50028	AX	в	N	NSSA	LA	Tiger
50029	AX	в	N	NSSA	LA	Renown
50030	AX	в	N	NWRA	OC	Repulse

Loc No	Dia	SC	Liv	Pool	Dep	Name
50031	AX			NWRA	OC	Hood
50032	AX		N	NWRA	OC	Courageous
50033	AX			NWRA	OC	Glorious
50034	AX		N	NWRA	OC	Furious
50035	AX	B	N	NWRA	OC	Ark Royal
50036	AX			NWRA	OC	Victorious
50037	AX		N	NWRA	OC	Illustrious
50039	AX			NWRA	OC	Implacable
50040	AX			NWRA	OC	Centurion
50041	AX	B	N	NSSA	LA	Bulwark
50042	AX			DCWA	LA	Triumph
50043	AX	B	N	NSSA	LA	Eagle
50044	AX	B	N	NSSA	LA	Exeter
50045	AX			DCWA	LA	Achilles
50046	AX	B		NWRA	OC	Ajax
50048	AX	B	N	NSSA	LA	Dauntless
50050	AX	B	N	NWRA	OC	Fearless

CLASS 50/1   TYPE 4   CO-CO

Built: English Electric 1968.
Experimental modified Class 50/0 locomotive
using bogies and traction motors of Class
37/5 locomotive. Engine derated to 2,450hp.

Maximum operating speed: 80mph.
Standard equipment: As Class 50/0 and
Cab/shore Radio (B).
Diagram: 50-1AX.

Sectors:
Railfreight: **FTLL:** China Clay, Laira.
Livery: *Railfreight General.* Fx.

Loc No	Dia	SC	Liv	Pool	Dep	Name
50149	AX		Fx	FTLL	LA	Defiance

CLASS 56   TYPE 5   CO-CO

Built: 56001-30 at Electroputere (Romania); others at BREL, 1977-84.
Engine: GEC Ruston-Paxman 16cyl, 4-stroke, 16RK3CT of 3,250hp (2,460kW).
Power/control equipment: Six Brush TM73-62 traction motors; main alternator Brush BA1101A.
Dimensions: 63.5ft L × 9.2ft W × 13ft H.
Brake force: 60 tonnes.
Maximum tractive effort: 49,456lb (270kN).
Route availability: 7.
Fuel: 1,150gal.

Train brake: Air.
Maximum operating speed: 80mph.
Train heating: Not equipped.
Diagram: 56-0AA.
Bogies: *Electroputere:* 56001-41/43-60. *BR CP1:* 56042. *BR CP2:* 56061-56135.
Standard equipment: Multiple working (Red Diamond, Code 3), Headlight (L), One man operation (M), Slow speed control (S), Sanding gear.
Special characteristics: Cab-shore radio (B). Remote control (Z).

Sectors:
Railfreight: **FALX:** Construction (Stone), Leicestershire. **FAWC:** Construction (Stone), Cardiff Canton. **FENB:** Coal, Midlands. **FEYA:** Coal, Yorkshire. **FEYB:** Coal, Blyth (Toton).

Loc No	Dia	SC	Liv	Pool	Dep
56001	AA	B	Fᴀ	FAWC	CF
Whatley					
56002	AA	B	F	FENB	TO
56003	AA	B		FENB	TO
56004	AA			FENB	TO
56005	AA		F	FENB	TO
56006	AA	B	F	FENB	TO
56007	AA	B	F	FENB	TO
56008	AA	B		FENB	TO
56009	AA	B	F	FENB	TO
56010	AA	B		FENB	TO
56011	AA	B	F	FENB	TO
56012	AA			FENB	TO
56013	AA	B		FENB	TO
56014	AA			FENB	TO
56015	AA			FENB	TO
56016	AA		F	FENB	TO
56017	AA		F	FENB	TO
56018	AA	B	F	FENB	TO
56019	AA			FENB	TO
56020	AA	B		FENB	TO
56021	AA	B		FENB	TO
56022	AA	B		FENB	TO
56023	AA			FENB	TO

Loc No	Dia	SC	Liv	Pool	Dep
56024	AA	B	F	FENB	TO
56025	AA	B		FENB	TO
56026	AA	B		FENB	TO
56027	AA			FENB	TO
56028	AA	B	Fᴇ	FENB	TO
West Burton Power Station					
56029	AA	B		FEYA	TO
56030	AA		Fᴇ	FEYA	TO
56031	AA			FAWC	CF
Merehead					
56032	AA			FAWC	CF
Sir de Morgannwg. County of South Glamorgan					
56033	AA		F	FAWC	CF
56034	AA		F	FAWC	CF
Castell Ogwr. Ogmore Castle					
56035	AA		F	FAWC	CF
Taff Merthyr					
56036	AA		Fᴘ	FAWC	CF
56037	AA		F	FAWC	CF
Richard Trevithick					

Loc No	Dia	SC	Liv	Pool	Dep
56038	AA		F	FAWC	CF
		Western Mail			
56039	AA	B	F	FAWC	CF
56040	AA	B	F	FAWC	CF
		Oystermouth			
56041	AA		F	FAWC	CF
56042	AA			FALX	TO
56043	AA		F	FAWC	CF
56044	AA		F	FAWC	CF
56045	AA	B	F	FAWC	CF
56046	AA		F	FAWC	CF
56047	AA	B		FEYA	TO
56048	AA			FAWC	CF
56049	AA	B	F	FAWC	CF
56050	AA		F	FAWC	CF
56051	AA		F	FAWC	CF
56052	AA		F	FAWC	CF
56053	AA		Fa	FAWC	CF
		Sir Morgannwg Ganol. County of Mid Glamorgan			
56054	AA			FEYA	TO
56055	AA		F	FAWC	CF
56056	AA		F	FAWC	CF
56057	AA		F	FAWC	CF
56058	AA	B	F	FALX	TO
56059	AA		F	FALX	TO
56060	AA	B	F	FALX	TO
56061	AA		F	FALX	TO
56062	AA		F	FALX	TO
56063	AA		F	FALX	TO
		Bardon Hill			
56064	AA		F	FALX	TO
56065	AA		F	FALX	TO
56066	AA		F	FEYA	TO
56067	AA		F	FEYA	TO
56068	AA		F	FEYA	TO
56069	AA			FEYA	TO
56070	AA			FALX	TO
56071	AA			FEYA	TO
56072	AA	Z		FAWC	CF
56073	AA	Z	Fe	FEYA	TO
56074	AA			FEYA	TO
		Kellingley Colliery			

Loc No	Dia	SC	Liv	Pool	Dep
56075	AA		F	FEYA	TO
		West Yorkshire Enterprise			
56076	AA		F	FEYA	TO
56077	AA		F	FEYA	TO
56078	AA		Fa	FALX	TO
56079	AA		F	FEYA	TO
56080	AA			FEYA	TO
56081	AA			FEYA	TO
56082	AA			FEYA	TO
56083	AA		F	FEYA	TO
56084	AA		F	FEYA	TO
56085	AA		F	FEYA	TO
56086	AA		F	FEYA	TO
56087	AA		F	FEYA	TO
56088	AA		F	FEYA	TO
56089	AA		F	FEYA	TO
56090	AA		F	FEYA	TO
56091	AA			FEYA	TO
56092	AA			FEYA	TO
56093	AA			FEYA	TO
56094	AA			FEYA	TO
56095	AA			FEYA	TO
		Harworth Colliery			
56096	AA		F	FEYA	TO
56097	AA		F-	FEYA	TO
56098	AA			FEYA	TO
56099	AA			FEYA	TO
56100	AA		F	FEYA	TO
56101	AA			FEYA	TO
56102	AA			FEYA	TO
56103	AA			FEYA	TO
56104	AA			FEYA	TO
56105	AA			FEYA	TO
56106	AA			FEYA	TO
56107	AA		F	FEYA	TO
56108	AA		F	FEYA	TO
56109	AA			FEYA	TO
56110	AA			FEYA	TO
56111	AA			FEYB	TO
56112	AA			FEYB	TO
56113	AA			FEYB	TO
56114	AA			FEYB	TO
56115	AA			FEYB	TO
56116	AA			FEYB	TO
56117	AA			FEYB	TO

Loc No	Dia	SC	Liv	Pool	Dep
56118	AA			FEYB	TO
56119	AA			FEYB	TO
56120	AA			FEYB	TO
56121	AA		FE	FEYB	TO
56122	AA		FE	FEYB	TO
Wilton Coal Power					
56123	AA		FE	FEYA	TO
Drax Power Station					
56124	AA			FEYB	TO
Blue Circle Cement					
56125	AA		FE	FEYB	TO
56126	AA			FEYB	TO
56127	AA			FEYB	TO
56128	AA			FEYB	TO

Loc No	Dia	SC	Liv	Pool	Dep
56129	AA			FEYB	TO
56130	AA			FEYB	TO
56131	AA			FEYB	TO
Ellington Colliery					
56132	AA			FEYB	TO
Fina Energy					
56133	AA			FEYB	TO
Crewe Locomotive Works					
56134	AA			FEYB	TO
Blyth Power					
56135	AA		F	FEYB	TO
Port of Tyne Authority					

CLASS 58   TYPE 5   CO-CO

Built: BREL 1983-85.
Engine: GEC Ruston Paxman 12cyl, 4-stroke, 12RK3ACT of 3,300hp (2,460kW).
Power/control equipment: Six Brush TM73-62 traction motors; main alternator Brush BA1101A.
Dimensions: 62.8ft L × 8.9ft W × 13.0ft H.
Brake force: 60 tonnes.
Maximum tractive effort: 60,750lb (329kN).

Route availability: 7.
Train brake: Air.
Maximum operating speed: 80mph.
Train heating: Not equipped.
Diagram: 58-OAA.
Standard equipment: Snowplough brackets (κ); Headlights (ʟ); One man operation (м); Slow speed control (s).

Sectors:
Railfreight: **FENA:** Coal, West Midlands. **FENC:** Coal, East Midlands.

Loc No	Dia	SC	Liv	Pool	Dep
58001	AA	B	F	FENA	TO
58002	AA	B	FE	FENC	TO
Daw Mill Colliery					
58003	AA	B	FE	FENA	TO
58004	AA		F	FENA	TO
58005	AA	B	F	FENA	TO
58006	AA		F	FENA	TO
58007	AA	B	F	FENA	TO

Loc No	Dia	SC	Liv	Pool	Dep
58008	AA	B	F	FENC	TO
58009	AA	B	F	FENA	TO
58010	AA	B	F	FENA	TO
58011	AA	B	F	FENA	TO
58012	AA	B	F	FENA	TO
58013	AA	B	F	FENA	TO
58014	AA	B	FE	FENA	TO
Didcot Power Station					

Loc No	Dia	SC	Liv	Pool	Dep
58015	AA	B	F	FENA	TO
58016	AA		F	FENC	TO
58017	AA	B	F	FENC	TO
58018	AA	B	Fe	FENC	TO

High Marnham Power Station

Loc No	Dia	SC	Liv	Pool	Dep
58019	AA	B	F	FENC	TO
58020	AA	B	F	FENC	TO

Doncaster Works

Loc No	Dia	SC	Liv	Pool	Dep
58021	AA	B	F	FENC	TO
58022	AA	B	F	FENC	TO
58023	AA	B	F	FENC	TO
58024	AA	B	F	FENC	TO
58025	AA	B	F	FENC	TO
58026	AA		F	FENC	TO
58027	AA		F	FENC	TO
58028	AA	B	F	FENC	TO
58029	AA	B	F	FENC	TO
58030	AA	B	F	FENC	TO
58031	AA		F	FENC	TO
58032	AA	B	F	FENC	TO
58033	AA		F	FENC	TO
58034	AA	B	F	FENC	TO

Bassetlaw

Loc No	Dia	SC	Liv	Pool	Dep
58035	AA		F	FENC	TO

Loc No	Dia	SC	Liv	Pool	Dep
58036	AA	B	F	FENC	TO
58037	AA		F	FENC	TO
58038	AA		F	FENC	TO
58039	AA		F	FENC	TO

Rugeley Power Station

Loc No	Dia	SC	Liv	Pool	Dep
58040	AA	B	F	FENC	TO

Cottam Power Station

Loc No	Dia	SC	Liv	Pool	Dep
58041	AA	B	Fe	FENC	TO

Ratcliffe Power Station

Loc No	Dia	SC	Liv	Pool	Dep
58042	AA	B	F	FENC	TO

Ironbridge Power Station

Loc No	Dia	SC	Liv	Pool	Dep
58043	AA		F	FENC	TO
58044	AA		F	FENC	TO
58045	AA		F	FENC	TO
58046	AA	B	F	FENC	TO
58047	AA		F	FENC	TO
58048	AA		F	FENC	TO
58049	AA	B	F	FENC	TO

Littleton Colliery

Loc No	Dia	SC	Liv	Pool	Dep
58050	AA		Fe	FENC	TO

Toton Traction Depot

CLASS 59	TYPE 5	CO-CO

Privately owned by Foster Yeoman Ltd, Merehead, Somerset

Built: General Motors, USA, 1985.
Engine: General Motors 16cyl, 4-stroke, 645E3C of 3,300hp (2,460kW).
Power/Control equipment: Six EMD D77B traction motors, main alternator EMD AR11 MLD D14A.
Weight: 126 tonnes.
Dimensions: 70.0ft L × 8.7ft W × 12.8ft H.
Brake force: 69 tonnes.
Maximum tractive effort: 122,000lb (573kN).

Sectors:
Private Owner: CYPO: Foster Yeoman.
Livery: Foster Yeoman Blue.

Route availability: 7.
Fuel: 990gal.
Train brakes: Air.
Maximum speed: 60mph.
Train heating: Not equipped.
Diagram: 59-0AA.
Standard equipment: Headlight (L); One man operation (M); Multiple working (within Class only), Sanding gear.
Special characteristics: Bell, No 1 end cab front, No 59001.

Loc No	Dia	SC	Liv	Pool	Dep	Name
59001	AA		★	CYPO	HQ	Yeoman Endeavous
59002	AA		★	CYPO	HQ	Yeoman Enterprise
59003	AA		★	CYPO	HQ	Yeoman Highlander
59004	AA		★	CYPO	HQ	Yeoman Challenger
59005			★	CYPO		

Note: Maintained at Merehead by BR staff.

CLASS 60   TYPE 5   CO-CO

Built: Brush Traction 1989-91.
Engine: Mirrlees Blackstone 8cyl, 4-stroke, 8MB875T of 3,100hp (kW).
Power/control equipment: Six Brush traction motors, main alternator
Weight: 126 tonnes.
Dimensions: ft L × ft W × ft H.
Brake Force: tonnes.

Maximum tractive effort: .
Route availability:
Fuel: gal.
Train brake: Air.
Maximum speed: 60mph.
Train heating: Not equipped.
Diagram: 60-0AA.
Standard equipment: Headlight (L), One man operation (M).

Sector:
Railfreight: **FA--:** Construction, Toton; **FP--:** Petroleum, Immingham.

Loc No	Dia	SC	Liv	Pool	Dep		Loc No	Dia	SC	Liv	Pool	Dep
60001	AA			F----	--		60019	AA			F----	--
60002	AA			F----	--		60020	AA			F----	--
60003	AA			F----	--		60021	AA			F----	--
60004	AA			F----	--		60022	AA			F----	--
60005	AA			F----	--		60023	AA			F----	--
60006	AA			F----	--		60024	AA			F----	--
60007	AA			F----	--		60025	AA			F----	--
60008	AA			F----	--		60026	AA			F----	--
60009	AA			F----	--		60027	AA			F----	--
60010	AA			F----	--		60028	AA			F----	--
60011	AA			F----	--		60029	AA			F----	--
60012	AA			F----	--		60030	AA			F----	--
60013	AA			F----	--		60031	AA			F----	--
60014	AA			F----	--		60032	AA			F----	--
60015	AA			F----	--		60033	AA			F----	--
60016	AA			F----	--		60034	AA			F----	--
60017	AA			F----	--		60035	AA			F----	--
60018	AA			F----	--		60036	AA			F----	--

Loc No	Dia	SC	Liv	Pool	Dep	Loc No	Dia	SC	Liv	Pool	Dep
60037	AA			F----	--	60069	AA			F----	--
60038	AA			F----	--	60070	AA			F----	--
60039	AA			F----	--	60071	AA			F----	--
60040	AA			F----	--	60072	AA			F----	--
60041	AA			F----	--	60073	AA			F----	--
60042	AA			F----	--	60074	AA			F----	--
60043	AA			F----	--	60075	AA			F----	--
60044	AA			F----	--	60076	AA			F----	--
60045	AA			F----	--	60077	AA			F----	--
60046	AA			F----	--	60078	AA			F----	--
60047	AA			F----	--	60079	AA			F----	--
60048	AA			F----	--	60080	AA			F----	--
60049	AA			F----	--	60081	AA			F----	--
60050	AA			F----	--	60082	AA			F----	--
60051	AA			F----	--	60083	AA			F----	--
60052	AA			F----	--	60084	AA			F----	--
60053	AA			F----	--	60085	AA			F----	--
60054	AA			F----	--	60086	AA			F----	--
60055	AA			F----	--	60087	AA			F----	--
60056	AA			F----	--	60088	AA			F----	--
60057	AA			F----	--	60089	AA			F----	--
60058	AA			F----	--	60090	AA			F----	--
60059	AA			F----	--	60091	AA			F----	--
60060	AA			F----	--	60092	AA			F----	--
60061	AA			F----	--	60093	AA			F----	--
60062	AA			F----	--	60094	AA			F----	--
60063	AA			F----	--	60095	AA			F----	--
60064	AA			F----	--	60096	AA			F----	--
60065	AA			F----	--	60097	AA			F----	--
60066	AA			F----	--	60098	AA			F----	--
60067	AA			F----	--	60099	AA			F----	--
60068	AA			F----	--	60100	AA			F----	--

CLASS 73/0   TYPE E   BO-BO

Built: British Railways 1962.
Dimensions: 53.7ft L × 8.7ft W × 12.5ft H.
Traction motors: Four English Electric EE542A.
Weight: 76.3 tonnes.
Brake force: 31 tonnes.
Route availability: 6.
Maximum operating speed: 80mph.

Train brake: Air, Vacuum and Electro-Pneumatic.
Diagram: 73-0AX (SR Type JA).

DIESEL engine: English Electric 4-cyl, 4-stroke, 4SRKT Mk 2 of 600hp (422kW).
Main generator: English Electric EE824/3D.
Fuel: 340gal.

ELECTRIC supply: Third rail, 660-750V dc; 1,420 (1,060kW) rail hp.
Maximum tractive effort: *Diesel:* 34,100lb (151kN). *Electric:* 42,000lb (186kN).
Train heating: *Diesel:* Preheating only from main generator. *Electric:* 675V dc, 400amps.

ETH Index: *Electric:* 66.
Standard equipment: Multiple working (Blue Star), One man operation (м); Driver-Guard communication; Sanding gear.

Sectors:
Network SouthEast: **NSSB:** Solent and Sarum.
Special livery: *Light blue:* 73004/05.

Loc No	Dia	SC	Liv	Pool	Dep
73001	AX			NSSB	SL
73002	AX			NSSB	SL
73003	AX			NSSB	SL
73004	AX		★	NSSB	SL
The Bluebell Railway					

Loc No	Dia	SC	Liv	Pool	Dep
73005	AX		★	NSSB	SL
Mid-Hants Watercress Line					
73006	AX			NSSB	SL

CLASS 73/1   TYPE E   BO-BO

Built: English Electric 1965-67.
Dimensions, Route availability, Train brake, Brake force: As Class 73/0.
Traction motors: Four English Electric EE546/1B.
Weight: 76.8 tonnes.
Maximum operating speed: 90mph.
Diagram: 73-1AX (SR Type JB).

DIESEL engine: As Class 73/0.
Main generator: English Electric EE824/5D.
Fuel: 310gal.

ELECTRIC supply: As Class 73/0.
Maximum tractive effort: *Diesel:* 36,000lb (160kN). *Electric:* 40,000lb (179kN).
Train heating: *Diesel:* Not equipped. *Electric:* As Class 73/0. Some to be modified to provide facilities as Class 73/0.
Standard equipment: As Class 73/0 plus flash guards for Gatwick Express service operation.

Sectors:
Departmental: **DCSA:** DCE Southern Region.
Railfreight: **FALS:** Construction (Stone), Stewarts Lane.
InterCity: **IVGA:** Victoria-Gatwick Express.
Network SouthEast: **NSSB:** Solent and Sarum, Stewarts Lane.

Loc No	Dia	SC	Liv	Pool	Dep
73101	AX		I	DCSA	SL
Brighton Evening Argos					
73103	AX		I	DCSA	SL
73104	AX			NSSB	SL
73105	AX		I	DCSA	SL
Quadrant					
73106	AX		I	NSSB	SL
73107	AX		I	NSSB	SL
73108	AX		I	DCSA	SL
73109	AX		I	DCSA	SL
73110	AX		I	DCSA	SL
73111	AX		I	NSSB	SL
73112	AX		I	NSSB	SL
73114	AX			DCSA	SL
73117	AX		I	DCSA	SL
University of Surrey					
73118	AX		I	DCSA	SL
The Romney Hythe and Dymchurch Railway					
73119	AX		I	DCSA	SL
Kentish Mercury					
73126	AX		I	DCSA	SL
73128	AX		I	DCSA	SL
73129	AX		I	DCSA	SL
City of Winchester					
73130	AX		I	DCSA	SL
City of Portsmouth					
73131	AX		I	DCSA	SL
County of Surrey					
73132	AX		I	DCSA	SL
73133	AX		I	DCSA	SL
73134	AX		I	DCSA	SL
Woking Homes 1885-1985					

Loc No	Dia	SC	Liv	Pool	Dep
73135	AX		I	DCSA	SL
73136	AX		I	NSSB	SL
73138	AX			NSSB	SL
73139	AX		I	NSSB	SL
73140	AX			NSSB	SL
73141	AX		I	FALS	SL
73201	AX		I	IVGA	SL
Broadlands					
73202	AX		I	IVGA	SL
Royal Observer Corps					
73203	AX		I	IVGA	SL
73204	AX		I	IVGA	SL
Stewarts Lane 1860-1985					
73205	AX		I	IVGA	SL
London Chamber of Commerce					
73206	AX		I	IVGA	SL
Gatwick Express					
73207	AX		I	IVGA	SL
County of East Sussex					
73208	AX		I	IVGA	SL
Croydon 1883-1983					
73209	AX		I	IVGA	SL
73210	AX		I	IVGA	SL
Selhurst					
73211	AX		I	IVGA	SL
County of West Sussex					
73212	AX		I	IVGA	SL
Airtour Suisse					

CLASS 81   TYPE A   BO-BO

Built: Birmingham Railway C&W 1960-61.
Supply system: Overhead Electric 25kV ac.
Dimensions: 56.5ft L × 8.7ft W × 13.0ft H
  (Pantograph housed).
Weight: 79.4 tonnes.
Traction motors: Four AEI Type 189 bogie
  suspension; Alsthom flexible, single reduction
  gear drive.
Control system: LT tap changing.
Maximum tractive effort: 50,000lb (222kN).

Train brakes: Auto air and air continuous
  vacuum.
Brake force: 40 tonnes.
Maximum operating speed: 80mph
  (originally 100mph).
Train heating: Electric, 320kW at 800V ac.
ETH Index: 66.
Diagram: 81-OBX.
Standard equipment: One man operation
  (M), Sanding gear.

Sectors:
InterCity: **IWCA:** West Coast main line.
Railfreight: **FGXZ:** Distribution (Speedlink) ac locomotives. **FMXX:** Metals, ac locomotives. **FXXL:**
  General.
Freightliner: **LXXA:** Distribution (Freightliner), General.
Parcels: **RXLE:** General.

Loc No	Dia	SC	Liv	Pool	Dep	Loc No	Dia	SC	Liv	Pool	Dep
81002	BX			*IWCA*	GW	81010	BX			*LXXA*	GW
81004	BX			*FMXX*	GW	81011	BX			*IWCA*	GW
81005	BX			*IWCA*	GW	81012	BX			*LXXA*	GW
81006	BX			*RXLE*	GW	81013	BX			*FGXZ*	GW
81007	BX			*LXXA*	GW	81017	BX			*FGXZ*	GW
81009	BX			*FMXX*	GW	81019	BX			*FXXL*	GW

CLASS 83   TYPE A   BO-BO

Built: English Electric 1961.
Supply system: Overhead Electric 25kV ac.
Dimensions: 52.5ft L × 8.7ft W × 13.0ft H
  (Pantograph housed).
Weight: 76.4 tonnes.
Traction motors: Four English Electric EE535A
  bogie suspension; SLM flexible single
  reduction gear drive.
Control system: LT tap changing.
Maximum tractive effort: 38,000lb.

Train brakes: Auto air and air continuous
  vacuum.
Brake force: 38 tonnes.
Maximum operating speed: 40mph
  (originally 100mph).
Train heating: Electric, 320kW at 800V ac.
ETH Index: 66.
Diagram: 83-OAX.
Standard equipment: One man operation
  (M), Sanding gear.

Sectors:
InterCity: **IWCA:** West Coast main line.
Note: Restricted to operation of empty coaching stock between Euston and Wembley InterCity CSD.

Loc No	Dia	SC	Liv	Pool	Dep
83009	AX			IWCA	WN
83012	AX			IWCA	WN

CLASS 85	TYPE A	BO-BO

Built: British Railways 1961-64.
Supply system: Overhead Electric 25kV ac.
Dimensions: 56.5ft L × 8.7ft W × 13.0ft H (Pantograph housed).
Weight: 82.5 tonnes.
Traction motors: Four AEI Type 189 bogie suspension; Alsthom flexible, single reduction drive system.
Control system: LT tap changing.
Rectifier: Silicon.
Maximum tractive effort: 50,000lb (222kN).
Train brakes: Auto air and air continuous vacuum.

Locomotive brakes: Straight air, auto air and rheostatic.
Brake force: 41 tonnes.
Maximum operating speed: 100mph (see SC).
Train heating: Electric, 320kW at 800V ac.
ETH Index: 66.
Diagram: 85-0AX.
Standard equipment: One man operation (M), Sanding gear.
Special characteristics: Maximum permitted speed 80mph (80).

Sectors:
Railfreight: **FGXZ:** Distribution (Speedlink) ac locomotives. **FXXL:** General.
InterCity: **IWCA:** West Coast main line.
Freightliner: **LXXA:** Distribution (Freightliner), General.
Network SouthEast: **NXXA:** General.
Parcels: **RXLE:** General.

Loc No	Dia	SC	Liv	Pool	Dep	Loc No	Dia	SC	Liv	Pool	Dep
85002	AX			RXLE	CE	85014	AX			RXLE	CE
85003	AX			NXXA	CE	85015	AX	80		FGXZ	CE
85004	AX	80		FGXZ	CE	85016	AX	80		FGXZ	CE
85005	AX	80		IWCA	CE	85018	AX	80		FGXZ	CE
85006	AX			FXXL	CE	85019	AX			RXLE	CE
85007	AX	80		LXXA	CE	85020	AX	80		FGXZ	CE
85008	AX			IWCA	CE	85021	AX	80		FGXZ	CE
85009	AX	80		FGXZ	CE	85022	AX			RXLE	CE
85010	AX	80		FGXZ	CE	85023	AX			RXLE	CE
85011	AX			RXLE	CE	85024	AX	80		FGXZ	CE
85012	AX	80		FGXZ	CE	85025	AX			RXLE	CE
85013	AX			FXXL	CE	85026	AX	80		FGXZ	CE

Loc No	Dia	SC	Liv	Pool	Dep		Loc No	Dia	SC	Liv	Pool	Dep
85028	AX			FGXZ	CE		85035	AX			FGXZ	CE
85030	AX	80		IWCA	CE		85036	AX			FXXL	CE
85031	AX	80		FGXZ	CE		85037	AX	80		IWCA	CE
85032	AX	80		FGXZ	CE		85038	AX	80		IWCA	CE
85034	AX	80		LXXA	CE		85040	AX	80		FGXZ	CE

CLASS 86/1   TYPE A   BO-BO

Built: English Electric 1965-66 as Class 86. Modified BREL Crewe 1972.
Supply System: Overhead electric 25kV ac.
Dimensions: 58.5ft L × 8.7ft W × 13.0ft H (Pantograph housed).
Weight: 86.8 tonnes.
Traction Motors: Four GEC type G412AZ, nose suspension, single reduction gear drive.
Control system: LT tap changing.
Performance: 5,000hp continuous rating.
Rectifier: Silicon.
Maximum tractive effort: 58,000lb (258kN).
Train brakes: Auto air and air continuous vacuum.

Locomotive brakes: Straight air, auto air and rheostatic.
Brake force: 40 tonnes.
Route availability: 6.
Maximum operating speed: 110mph.
Train heating: 320kW at 800V ac.
ETH Index: 66 (95 on stock with 600amp wiring).
Diagram: 86-1BX.
Standard equipment: BP9 bogies with flexicoil springs; One man operation (M); Driver/guard communication; Sanding gear.
Special characteristics: Headlight (L).

Sector:
InterCity: **IWCA:** West Coast main line.
Livery: InterCity.

Loc No	Dia	SC	Liv	Pool	Dep	Name
86101	BX	L	I	IWCA	WN	Sir William A. Stanier FRS
86102	BX		I	IWCA	WN	Robert A. Riddles
86103	BX	LL	I	IWCA	WN	André Chapelon

CLASS 86/2   TYPE A   BO-BO

Built: British Railways (†) and English Electric 1965-66.
Supply System, Dimensions, Control system, Rectifier, Maximum tractive effort, Train brakes, Locomotive brakes,

Brake force, Route availability, Train heating, all as Class 86/1.
Traction Motors: Four AEI type 282AZ, nose suspension, single reduction gear drive.
Performance: 4,040hp continuous rating.
ETH Index: 66.

65

Diagram	Weight	Max speed
86-2BX	85.0 tonnes	100mph
86-2CX	86.2 tonnes	100mph
	Ballast weighted bogies	
86-2DX	85.0 tonnes	110mph
86-2EX	86.2 tonnes	110mph
	Ballast weighted bogies	

Standard equipment: One man operation (M); Driver/guard communication; Sanding gear.
Special characteristics: Cab/shore radio (B); Headlight (L); Push-pull (Time Division Multiplex system (P).

Sectors:
InterCity: **IANA:** Anglia Region. **ICCA:** Cross-Country. **ICHA:** Charter. **IWCA:** West Coast main line. **IWCB:** West Coast main line (equipped TDM).
Freightliner: **LXXA:** Railfreight Distribution (Freightliner), General.
Network SouthEast: **NXXA:** General.
Parcels: **RXLE:** General.

Loc No	Dia	SC	Liv	Pool	Dep	Name
86204	BX		I	ICHA	WN	City of Carlisle
86206	CX			ICCA	WN	City of Stoke on Trent
86207	BX		I	ICCA	WN	City of Lichfield
86208	CX		I	IWCA	WN	City of Chester
86209†	EX	L	I	IWCA	WN	City of Coventry
86210	CX	L	I	ICCA	WN	City of Edinburgh
86212	CX		I	IWCB	WN	Preston Guild
86213	CX	L	I	RXLE	WN	Lancashire Witch
86214†	BX	L	I	IANA	WN	Sans Pareil
86215	BX		I	IANA	WN	Joseph Chamberlain
86216	BX	L	I	IANA	WN	Meteor
86218	BX		I	IANA	WN	Planet
86219	CX		I	IWCB	WN	Phoenix
86220	CX		I	IANA	WN	The Round Tabler
86221†	CX		I	IANA	WN	BBC Look East
86223	CX		I	IANA	WN	Norwich Union
86224†	EX	B	I	IWCA	WN	Caledonian
86225	DX	BL	I	RXLE	WN	Hardwicke
86226	BX		I	IWCA	WN	Royal Mail Midlands
86227†	BX		I	IANA	WN	Sir Henry Johnson
86228	BX	P	I	IWCB	WN	Vulcan Heritage
86229†	BX	L	I	IANA	WN	Sir John Betjeman
86230	BX	L	I	IANA	WN	The Duke of Wellington
86231†	EX		I	IWCB	WN	Starlight Express
86232†	BX		I	IANA	WN	Harold Macmillan
86234	CX		I	RXLE	WN	J. B. Priestley O.M.
86235	CX		I	IANA	WN	Novelty

Loc No	Dia	SC	Liv	Pool	Dep	Name
86236†	CX	L	I	IWCA	WN	Josiah Wedgwood. Master Potter 1730-1795
86237	CX		I	IANA	WN	Sir Charles Hallé
86238†	BX	L	I	IANA	WN	European Community
86239	BX	B		IWCA	WN	L. S. Lowry
86240†	CX	PL	I	IWCB	WN	Bishop Eric Treacy
86241†	BX			IWCB	WN	Glenfiddich
86242†	CX		I	RXLE	WN	James Kennedy GC
86243	CX		I	RXLE	WN	The Boys' Brigade
86244	BX		I	IANA	WN	The Royal British Legion
86245	CX	L	I	RXLE	WN	Dudley Castle
86247	CX		I	ICCA	WN	Abraham Darby
86248†	BX	L	I	ICCA	WN	Sir Clwyd — County of Clwyd
86249	BX			NXXA	WN	County of Merseyside
86250	CX	L	I	ICCA	WN	The Glasgow Herald
86251	CX	B	I	IWCA	WN	The Birmingham Post
86252†	BX	B	I	IWCA	WN	The Liverpool Daily Post
86253†	CX		I	ICCA	WN	The Manchester Guardian
86254	CX		I	RXLE	WN	William Webb Ellis
86255	CX		I	ICCA	WN	Penrith Beacon
86256†	CX		I	ICHA	WN	Pebble Mill
86257†	CX	L	I	NXXA	WN	Snowdon
86259†	CX	L	I	IANA	WN	Peter Pan
86260	CX		I	IANA	WN	Driver Wallace Oakes G.C.
86261†	BX		I	NXXA	WN	Driver John Axon G.C.

CLASS 86/4   TYPE A   BO-BO

Built: British Railways (†) and English Electric 1965-66.
Supply System, Dimensions, Control system, Rectifier, Maximum tractive effort, Train brakes, Locomotive brakes, Brake force, Route availability, Train heating, all as Class 86/1.
Traction Motors: Four GEC type G412BZ, nose suspension, single reduction gear drive.
Performance: As Class 86/2.
Maximum speed: 100mph.
ETH Index: 66.

Diagram	Weight	
86-4AX	83.0 tonnes	
86-4BX	83.9 tonnes	Ballast weighted bogies

Standard equipment: Flexicoil suspension and SAB wheels; Multiple working only with other locomotives fitted with 36-way jumper cables (Class 86/4 & 87) and others with TDM(P) equipment. One man operation (M); Driver/guard communication; Sanding gear.
Special characteristics: Cab/shore radio (B); Headlight (L).

Sectors:
Railfreight: **FGXZ:** Distribution (Speedlink), ac locomotives. **FMXX:** Metals. **FVXX:** Metals (Automotive).
InterCity: **ICCA:** Cross-Country. **IWCA:** West Coast main line.
Freightliner: **LXXA:** Railfreight Distribution (Freightliner), General.
Network SouthEast: **NXXA:** General.
Parcels: **RXLE:** General.
Special Livery: Electric blue 86426.

Loc No	Dia	SC	Liv	Pool	Dep	Name
86401	BX	LM	N	NXXA	WN	
86402	AX	LM		LXXA	WN	
86403†	AX	LM	I	LXXA	WN	
86404†	AX	LM	I	LXXA	WN	
86405	AX	M	I	IWCA	WN	
86406†	AX	LM	I	LXXA	WN	
86407	AX	LM	I	LXXA	WN	The Institution of Electrical Engineers
86408	BX	LM	I	LXXA	WN	St John Ambulance
86409†	AX	LM	I	LXXA	WN	
86410†	AX	LM	I	IWCA	WN	
86411	AX	M	I	LXXA	WN	Airey Neave
86412†	AX	LM	I	ICCA	WN	Elizabeth Garrett Anderson
86413†	BX	LM	I	FVXX	WN	County of Lancashire
86414	BX	LM	I	FVXX	WN	Frank Hornby
86415†	BX	LM	I	FMXX	WN	Rotary International
86416†	AX	LM	I	LXXA	WN	Wigan Pier
86417	BX	LM	I	LXXA	WN	The Kingsman
86418	AX	LM	I	FMXX	WN	
86419†	AX	LM	I	IWCA	WN	
86420†	AX	LM	I	LXXA	WN	
86421	BX	LM	I	LXXA	WN	London School of Economics
86422	AX	LM	I	FMXX	WN	
86423	BX	LM	I	FMXX	WN	
86424†	AX	LM	I	IWCA	WN	
86425	BX	LM	I	RXLE	WN	
86426	BX	LM	★	RXLE	WN	
86427†	AX	LM	I	FMXX	WN	The Industrial Society
86428	BX	M	I	IWCA	WN	Aldaniti
86430†	AX	LM	I	IWCA	WN	Scottish National Orchestra
86431	BX	M	I	IWCA	WN	
86432	BX	M	I	FMXX	WN	Brookside
86433	BX	M	I	FMXX	WN	Wulfruna
86434	AX		I	FGXZ	WN	University of London
86435†	BX		I	LXXA	WN	
86436	BX		I	FGXZ	WN	
86437†	BX		I	IWCA	WN	
86438†	AX	L	I	LXXA	WN	
86439	BX	L	I	ICCA	WN	

CLASS 86/5   TYPE A   BO-BO

Built: British Railways (†) and English Electric 1965-66. Regeared for Freightliner duties at BREL Crewe 1988/89.
Supply System, Dimensions, Traction motors, Control system, Performance, Rectifier, Maximum tractive effort, Train brakes, Locomotive brakes, Brake force, Route availability, Train heating, ETH Index, Standard equipment: all as Class 86/2.

Maximum speed: 75mph.

Diagram	Weight	
86-5AX	86.2 tonnes	Ballast weighted bogies
86-5BX	85.0 tonnes	

Special characteristics: Cab/shore radio (B); Headlight (L); Multiple Working (to be equipped).

Sector:
Freightliner: **LNRE:** Railfreight Distribution (Freightliner) West Coast main line ac locomotives.

Loc No	Dia	SC	Liv	Pool	Dep	Name
86501 (86258)†	AX	L	I	LNRE	WN	Talyllyn
86502 (86222)†	AX	B	Fx	LNRE	WN	Lloyd's List
86503 (86205)†	AX		F-	LNRE	WN	City of Lancaster
86504 (86217)	BX	B	F-	LNRE	WN	Halley's Comet
86505 (86246)	BX		F-	LNRE	WN	Royal Anglian Regiment
86506 (86233)	AX		F-	LNRE	WN	Laurence Olivier
86507 ( )						
86508 ( )						
86509 ( )						
86510 ( )						

CLASS 87/0   BO-BO

Built: BREL Crewe. 1973-74.
Supply System: Overhead electric 25kV ac.
Dimensions: 58.5ft L × 8.7ft W × 13.1ft H (Pantograph housed).
Weight: 83.3 tonnes.
Traction Motors: Four GEC type G412AZ fully suspended, single reduction gear drive.

Control system: HT tap changing.
Performance: 5,000hp continuous rating.
Rectifier: Silicon.
Maximum tractive effort: 58,000lb (258kN).
Train brakes: Air.

Locomotive brakes: Air and Rheostatic.
Brake force: 40 tonnes.
Route availability: 6.
Maximum operating speed: 110mph.
Train heating: 460kV A at 800V ac.
ETH Index: 74 (95 on stock with 600amp wiring).
Diagram: 87-0AA.

Standard equipment: Multiple Working with ac locomotives fitted with 36-way jumper cables (Class 86/4 & 87) and other with TDM(P) equipment; Driver/guard communication; Headlights (L); Sanding gear.
Special characteristics: Cab/shore radio (B).

Sectors:
InterCity: **ICCA:** Cross Country. **IWCA:** West Coast main line.
Freightliner: **LXXA:** Railfreight Distribution (Freightliner), General.

Loc No	Dia	SC	Liv	Pool	Dep	Name
87001	AA		I	IWCA	WN	Royal Scot
87002	AA		I	IWCA	WN	Royal Sovereign
87003	AA		I	IWCA	WN	Patriot
87004	AA		I	IWCA	WN	Britannia
87005	AA		I	LXXA	WN	City of London
87006	AA		I	LXXA	WN	Glasgow Garden Festival
87007	AA		I	IWCA	WN	City of Manchester
87008	AA		I	IWCA	WN	City of Liverpool
87009	AA		I	ICCA	WN	City of Birmingham
87010	AA	B	I	ICCA	WN	King Arthur
87011	AA		I	IWCA	WN	The Black Prince
87012	AA		I	IWCA	WN	The Royal Bank of Scotland
87013	AA		I	LXXA	WN	John o'Gaunt
87014	AA	B	I	IWCA	WN	Knight of the Thistle
87015	AA		I	IWCA	WN	Howard of Effingham
87016	AA		I	IWCA	WN	Sir Francis Drake
87017	AA		I	IWCA	WN	Iron Duke
87018	AA		I	IWCA	WN	Lord Nelson
87019	AA		I	IWCA	WN	Sir Winston Churchill
87020	AA		I	IWCA	WN	North Briton
87021	AA		I	IWCA	WN	Robert the Bruce
87022	AA		I	IWCA	WN	Cock o' the North
87023	AA		I	IWCA	WN	Velocity
87024	AA		I	IWCA	WN	Lord of the Isles
87025	AA		I	IWCA	WN	County of Cheshire
87026	AA		I	IWCA	WN	Sir Richard Arkwright
87027	AA		I	IWCA	WN	Wolf of Badenoch
87028	AA		I	IWCA	WN	Lord President
87029	AA		I	IWCA	WN	Earl Marischal
87030	AA		I	IWCA	WN	Black Douglas
87031	AA	B	I	ICCA	WN	Hal o' the Wynd
87032	AA		I	ICCA	WN	Kenilworth
87033	AA		I	IWCA	WN	Thane of Fife
87034	AA		I	IWCA	WN	William Shakespeare
87035	AA		I	IWCA	WN	Robert Burns

CLASS 87/1   BO-BO

Built: BREL Crewe 1975.
Supply System, Dimensions, Maximum tractive effort, Train brakes, Locomotive brakes, Brake force, Route availability, Standard equipment, ETH Index: as Class 87/0.
Weight: 79.1 tonnes.

Traction Motors: Four GEC type G412BZ fully suspended, single reduction gear drive.
Control system & Rectifier: Thyristor.
Performance: 4,850hp continuous rating.
Maximum operating speed: 110mph.
Train heating: 510kV A at 890V ac.
Diagram: 87-1AA.

Sector:
Railfreight: **FVXX:** Metals (Automotive).

Loc No	Dia	SC	Liv	Pool	Dep	Name
87101	AA			FVXX	WN	Stephenson

CLASS 89   CO-CO

Built: BREL Crewe (for Hawker-Siddeley) 1986.
Supply System: Overhead electric 25kV ac.
Dimensions: 64.9ft L × 9ft W × 13.0ft H (pantograph housed).
Weight: 104 tonnes.
Traction Motors: Brush.
Control system: Thyristor.
Performance: 5,830hp (4,350kW) continuous rating.
Rectifier: Thyristor.
Maximum tractive effort: 46,200lb (205kN).

Train brakes: Air.
Locomotive brakes: Air and Rheostatic.
Brake force: 50 tonnes.
Route availability: 6.
Maximum operating speed: 125mph.
Train heating: Electric, 510kVA at 890V ac.
ETH Index: 95.
Diagram: 89-0AA.
Standard equipment: Headlight (L); One man operation (M).

Sector:
InterCity: **IECA:** East Coast main line.
Livery: InterCity.

Loc No	Dia	SC	Liv	Pool	Dep
89001	AA		I	IECA	BN

CLASS 90   BO-BO

Built: BREL Crewe 1987-90.
Supply System: Overhead electric 25kV ac.
Dimensions: 61.5ft L × 9ft W × 13ft H
(pantograph housed).
Weight: 84.5 tonnes.
Traction Motors: Four GEC type G412BZ, fully
suspended, single reduction gear drive.
Control system: Microprocessor, air-cooled
Thyristor.
Performance: 4,850hp (3,260kW) continuous
rating.
Rectifier: Thyristor.
Maximum tractive effort: 192kN.

Train brakes: Air.
Locomotive brakes: Air and Rheostatic.
Brake force: 40 tonnes.
Route availability: 7.
Maximum operating speed: 110mph.
Train heating: Electric, 510kV A at 890V ac.
ETH Index: 95.
Diagram: 90-0AA
Standard equipment: Push-pull operation
(Time Division Multiplex system); Multiple
Working with ac locomotives SC P; Snowplough
brackets (K); Driver/guard communication;
Headlights (L); One man operation (M).

Sectors:
Railfreight: **FGXZ:** Distribution (Speedlink). **FMXX:** Metals.
InterCity: **IWCA:** West Coast main line.
Freightliner: **LXXA:** Railfreight Distribution (Freightliner).

Loc No	Dia	SC	Liv	Pool	Dep	Name
90001	AA	P	I	IWCA	WN	
90002	AA	P	I	IWCA	WN	
90003	AA	P	I	IWCA	WN	
90004	AA	P	I	IWCA	WN	
90005	AA	P	I	IWCA	WN	Financial Times
90006	AA	P	I	IWCA	WN	
90007	AA	P	I	IWCA	WN	
90008	AA	P	I	IWCA	WN	
90009	AA	P	I	IWCA	WN	
90010	AA	P	I	IWCA	WN	
90011	AA	P	I	IWCA	WN	Chartered Institute of Transport
90012	AA	P	I	IWCA	WN	
90013	AA	P	I	IWCA	WN	
90014	AA	P	I	IWCA	WN	
90015	AA	P	I	IWCA	WN	
90016	AA	P	I	FMXX	WN	
90017	AA	P	I	FMXX	WN	
90018	AA	P	I	IWCA	WN	
90019	AA	P	I	IWCA	WN	
90020	AA	P		IWCA		
90021	AA	P		IWCA		

Loc No	Dia	SC	Liv	Pool	Dep
90022	AA	P		IWCA	
90023	AA	P		FGXZ	
90024	AA	P		IWCA	
90025	AA	P		FGXZ	
90026	AA	P		FGXZ	
90027	AA	P		LXXA	
90028	AA	P		LXXA	
90029	AA	P		LXXA	

CLASS 91 · BO-BO

Built: GEC (constructed by BREL Crewe), 1988-90.
Supply system: Overhead electric 25kV ac.
Dimensions: 63.7ft L × 9ft W × 12.3ft H (Pantograph housed).
Weight: 84.1 tonnes.
Traction motors: GEC.
Control system: Microprocessor, air-cooled Thyristor.
Performance: 6,080hp (4,530kN) continuous rating.
Rectifier: Thyristor.
Maximum tractive effort: --lb (--kN).

Train brakes: Air.
Locomotive brakes: Air and Rheostatic.
Brake force: 45 tonnes.
Route availability: 7.
Maximum operating speed: 140mph.
Train heating: Electric, 510kV A at 890V ac.
ETH Index: 95.
Diagram: 91-0AA.
Standard equipment: Push-pull operation (Time Division Multiplex system); Multiple working with ac locomotives SC P; Driver/guard communication; Headlights (L); One man operation (M).

Sector:
InterCity: **IECA:** East Coast main line.
Livery: *InterCity.*

Loc No	Dia	SC	Liv	Pool	Dep
91001	AA	P	I	IECA	BN
91002	AA	P	I	IECA	BN
91003	AA	P	I	IECA	BN
91004	AA	P	I	IECA	BN
91005	AA	P	I	IECA	BN
91006	AA	P	I	IECA	BN
91007	AA	P	I	IECA	BN
91008	AA	P	I	IECA	BN
91009	AA	P	I	IECA	BN
91010	AA	P		IECA	
91011	AA	P		IECA	
91012	AA	P		IECA	
91013	AA	P		IECA	

Loc No	Dia	SC	Liv	Pool	Dep
91014	AA	P		IECA	
91015	AA	P		IECA	
91016	AA	P		IECA	
91017	AA	P		IECA	
91018	AA	P		IECA	
91019	AA	P		IECA	
91020	AA	P		IECA	
91021	AA	P		IECA	
91022	AA	P		IECA	
91023	AA	P		IECA	
91024	AA	P		IECA	
91025	AA	P		IECA	
91026	AA	P		IECA	
91027	AA	P		IECA	
91028	AA	P		IECA	
91029	AA	P		IECA	
91030	AA	P		IECA	
91031	AA	P		IECA	

InterCity 125 trains. Mk 3A Passenger Carrying Coaching Stock

Each set comprises a rake of between seven and nine Mk 3 coaches including a catering vehicle and a GJ2 (Trailer Guard Standard) having facilities for the travelling Conductor Guard.

Formations are generally semi-permanent to ensure regular maintenance schedules are adhered to, but temporary changes may be effected when a fault is found on a vehicle which cannot be rectified within the scheduled maintenance period. To provide cover a few spare vehicles are held at the main depots.

The coaches are not compatible with standard Mk 3 coaching stock. Movement is restricted to haulage by Class 43 locomotives (Power Cars) or buckeye coupling fitted Class 08 shunting locomotives unless an appropriate barrier coach with buckeye and conventional couplings is provided. To allow haulage of train sets by Push Pull fitted (Time Division Multiplex system) electric locomotives some TGS coaches are being modified with buffers and conventional coupling gear.

Standard data:
Built: BREL Derby Carriage Works 1976-82.
Dimensions: 23.0m L × 2.74m W × 3.81m H.
Maximum speed: 125mph.
Equipment: Air brakes, public address, electric heating and air conditioning, fluorescent and tungsten lighting.
Special characteristics: Public payphone (P). Refurbished (unless applicable to all of type) (R). Reference to smoking/non-smoking accommodation is only made where it is the only significant variation between diagrams.

Sectors:
INTERCITY: **ICC:** Cross Country. **ICH:** Charter. **IEC:** East Coast main line. **IML:** Midland Lines. **IWR:** Western Region.

Livery: All refurbished vehicles (R) carry *INTERCITY* livery, latest outshopped include the Swallow emblem introduced during 1988.

TRB: Trailer Restaurant with Buffet, Unclassified

Diagram: GN4.01.0A.
Weight: 38 tonnes.
Bogies: BT10 and BT10a (one each).

Equipment: Microwave/Microaire electric ovens, Public address transmitter.
Seats: 23.

Veh No	Dia	SC	Liv	Pool	Dep	Veh No	Dia	SC	Liv	Pool	Dep
40204	0A	R	I	IWR	PM	40209	0A	R	I	IWR	PM
40205	0A	R	I	IWR	PM	40210	0A			IWR	PM
40206	0A			IWR	PM	40211	0A			IWR	PM
40207	0A	R	I	IWR	PM	40212	0A	R	I	IWR	PM
40208	0A	R	I	IWR	PM	40213	0A	R	I	IWR	PM

TRUB: Trailer Restaurant Unclassified, Buffet

Diagram: GK4.01.0C.
Weight: 39 tonnes.
Bogies: BT10b and BT10c (one each).

Equipment: Microwave/Microaire electric ovens, Public address transmitter.
Seats: 17.

Veh No	Dia	SC	Liv	Pool	Dep	Veh No	Dia	SC	Liv	Pool	Dep
40322	0C	R		IWR	LA	40326	0C	R		IWR	LA
40323	0C	R		IWR	LA	40327	0C	R		IWR	LA
40324	0C	R		IWR	LA	40331	0C	R		IWR	LA
40325	0C	R		IWR	LA	40355	0C	R		IWR	LA

TRSB: Trailer Restaurant Standard with Buffet

Diagram: GK2.02.0B.
Weight: 36 tonnes.
Equipment: Microwave/Microaire electric ovens, Public address transmitter.

Bogies: One each BT10 and BT10a.
Seats: 35.

Veh No	Dia	SC	Liv	Pool	Dep		Veh No	Dia	SC	Liv	Pool	Dep
40401	0B	PR	I	ICC	PM		40425	0B	R	I	ICC	PM
40402	0B	PR	I	ICC	PM		40426	0B	R	I	ICC	LA
40403	0B	R	I	ICC	PM		40427	0B	R	I	IWR	OO
40414	0B	R	I	ICC	LA		40428	0B			IWR	PM
40415	0B	PR	I	ICC	LA		40429	0B		I	IEC	NL
40416	0B	R	I	IWR	OO		40430	0B	PR	I	ICC	LA
40417	0B	R	I	IWR	OO		40431	0B	P		ICC	LA
40418	0B	R	I	IWR	OO		40432	0B			ICC	LA
40419	0B	R	I	IWR	OO		40433	0B			ICC	LA
40420	0B	R	I	IWR	PM		40434	0B			ICC	LA
40421	0B	P		ICC	PM		40435	0B	R	I	IWR	PM
40422	0B	R	I	IWR	PM		40436	0B	R	I	IWR	OO
40423	0B	R	I	IWR	OO		40437	0B	R	I	IWR	OO
40424	0B	R	I	IWR	LA							

TRFK: Trailer Restaurant First (Pullman) with Kitchen

Diagram: GL1.01.0A.
Weight: 37 tonnes.
Equipment: Microwave/Microaire ovens,
Public address transmitter.

Bogies: One each BT10 and BT10a.
Seats: 24.

Veh No	Dia	SC	Liv	Pool	Dep
40501	0A	R	I	IEC	NL
40505	0A	R	I	IEC	NL
40511	0A	R	I	IEC	NL

TLUK: Trailer Lounge Unclassifed with Kitchen

Modified from TRFK in 1984. Available for special hire as additional or replacement in standard train.

Diagram: GM4.01.0A.
Weight: 36.5 tonnes.
Equipment: Microwave/Microaire ovens.
Bogies: One each BT10 and BT10a.

Seats: 16 (eight at conference table, eight lounge chairs).
Toilet: 1.

Veh No	Dia	SC	Liv	Pool	Dep
40513	0A	R	I	ICH	BN

TRFM: Trailer Restaurant First, Modular

Modified from TRFB in 1987. Operated in Sheffield-St Pancras 'Master Cutler' service.

Diagram: GK1.02.0A.
Weight: 39 tonnes.
Equipment: Microwave/Microaire ovens
  (Cuisine 2000 Modular catering); Public
  address transmitter.

Bogies: One each BT10 and BT10a.
Seats: 17.
Toilet: 1 (staff).

Veh No	Dia	SC	Liv	Pool	Dep
40619	0A	R	I	IML	NL

TRFB: Trailer Restaurant First with Buffet

Diagram	Weight	Bogies (one each)
GH1.01.0A	38 tonnes	BT10 and BT10a
GK1.01.0B	39 tonnes	BT10b and BT10c

Equipment: Microwave/Microaire ovens; Public address transmitter.
Seats: 17.

Veh No	Dia	SC	Liv	Pool	Dep		Veh No	Dia	SC	Liv	Pool	Dep
40700	0A	PR	I	IEC	NL		40721	0A	R	I	IEC	BN
40701	0A	PR	I	IEC	BN		40728	0B	PR	I	IEC	NL
40702	0A	PR	I	IEC	BN		40729	0B	R	I	IEC	BN
40703	0A	PR	I	IEC	BN		40730	0B	PR	I	IEC	NL
40704	0A	R	I	IEC	BN		40732	0B	PR	I	IWR	LA
40705	0A	PR	I	IEC	BN		40733	0B	PR	I	IEC	BN
40706	0A	PR	I	IEC	BN		40734	0B	PR	I	IEC	BN
40707	0A	R	I	IEC	BN		40735	0B	P	I	IML	NL
40708	0A	R	I	IEC	BN		40736	0B	P	I	IEC	BN
40709	0A	PR	I	IML	NL		40737	0B	P	I	IML	NL
40710	0A	PR	I	IEC	BN		40738	0B	PR	I	IML	NL
40711	0A	P	I	IEC	NL		40739	0B	PR	I	IEC	BN
40712	0A	PR	I	IEC	NL		40740	0B		I	IEC	BN
40713	0A	PR	I	IEC	NL		40741	0B	PR	I	IML	NL
40714	0A	PR	I	IEC	NL		40742	0B	R	I	IEC	BN
40715	0A	PR	I	IEC	BN		40743	0B	P	I	IML	NL
40716	0A	R	I	IEC	BN		40744	0B	P	I	IML	NL
40717	0A	R	I	IEC	BN		40745	0B	PR	I	IML	NL
40718	0A	PR	I	IEC	BN		40746	0B	PR	I	IML	NL
40720	0A	R	I	IEC	BN		40747	0B	P	I	IML	NL

Veh No	Dia	SC	Liv	Pool	Dep		Veh No	Dia	SC	Liv	Pool	Dep
40748	0B		I	IML	NL		40753	0B	P	I	IEC	NL
40749	0B	PR	I	IEC	HT		40754	0B	R	I	IEC	BN
40750	0B	P		IML	NL		40756	0B	R	I	IEC	BN
40751	0B	PR	I	IEC	NL		40757	0B	PR	I	IWR	LA
40752	0B			IEC	NL							

TF: Trailer First

Diagram	Weight	Bogies	Variation
GH1.02.0A	33 tonnes	BT10	
GH1.02.0B	33.5 tonnes	BT10b	
GH1.02.0D	33.5 tonnes	BT10b	Refurbished
GH1.02.0E	33 tonnes	BT10	All non-smoking
GH1.02.0F	33.5 tonnes	BT10b	All non-smoking
GH1.02.1C	33 tonnes	BT10	Converted prototype
GH1.02.1G	33 tonnes	BT10	Converted prototype, all non-smoking
GH1.02.2A	33 tonnes	BT10	Payphone
GH1.02.2B	33.5 tonnes	BT10b	Payphone
GH1.02.2D	33.5 tonnes	BT10b	Refurbished, Payphone
GH1.02.0E	33 tonnes	BT10	All non-smoking, Payphone
GH1.02.3A	34 tonnes	BT10	
GH1.02.3B	34 tonnes	BT10	All non-smoking

Equipment: One table and seat removable for disabled passengers.   **Seats:** 48.   **Toilets:** 2.

Veh No	Dia	SC	Liv	Pool	Dep		Veh No	Dia	SC	Liv	Pool	Dep
41003	2A	PR	I	IWR	PM		41020	0E			IWR	PM
41004	0E	R	I	IWR	PM		41021	2A	P		IWR	PM
41005	2A	PR	I	IWR	PM		41022	0E			IWR	PM
41006	0E	R	I	IWR	PM		41023	2A	PR	I	IWR	LA
41007	2A	PR	I	IWR	PM		41024	0E	R	I	IWR	LA
41008	0E	R	I	IWR	PM		41025	2A	PR	I	IWR	LA
41009	2A	PR	I	IWR	PM		41026	0E	R	I	IWR	LA
41010	0E	R	I	IWR	PM		41027	2A	PR	I	IWR	LA
41011	2A	PR	I	IWR	PM		41028	0E	R	I	IWR	LA
41012	0E	R	I	IWR	PM		41029	2A	PR	I	IWR	LA
41013	2A	P		IWR	PM		41030	0E	R	I	IWR	LA
41014	0E			IWR	PM		41031	2A	PR	I	IWR	LA
41015	2A	P	I	IWR	PM		41032	0E	R	I	IWR	LA
41016	0E		I	IWR	PM		41033	2A	PR	I	IWR	LA
41017	2A	P	I	IWR	PM		41034	0E	R	I	IWR	LA
41018	0E		I	IWR	PM		41035	0A	PR	I	IWR	OO
41019	2A	P		IWR	PM		41036	0E	R	I	IWR	OO

Veh No	Dia	SC	Liv	Pool	Dep
41037	2A	PR	I	IWR	OO
41038	0E	R	I	IWR	OO
41039	0E			IML	NL
41040	0E			IML	NL
41041	2E	PR	I	IEC	NL
41042	0A	R	I	ICC	LA
41043	0A	R	I	IML	NL
41044	0E	R	I	IML	NL
41045	0A	R	I	IML	NL
41046	0A	R	I	IEC	BN
41047	0A			IML	NL
41048	0E			IML	NL
41049	0A	R	I	IML	NL
41050	0E	R	I	IML	NL
41051	0A	R	I	IML	NL
41052	0E	R	I	IML	NL
41053	0A			IML	NL
41054	0E			IML	NL
41055	0A	R	I	IML	NL
41056	0E	R	I	IML	NL
41057	0A	R	I	IEC	BN
41058	0E	R	I	IEC	BN
41059	0A	R	I	IEC	BN
41060	0E	R	I	IEC	BN
41061	0A	R	I	IEC	BN
41062	0E	R	I	IEC	BN
41063	0A	R	I	IEC	BN
41064	0E	R	I	IEC	BN
41065	0A	R	I	IML	NL
41066	2E	P		IEC	HT
41067	0A	R	I	IEC	NL
41068	0E	R	I	IEC	NL
41069	0A	R	I	IEC	NL
41070	0E	R	I	IEC	NL
41071	0A	R	I	IEC	NL
41072	0E	R	I	IEC	NL
41073	0A			IEC	NL
41074	0E			IEC	NL
41075	0A	R	I	IEC	BN
41076	0E	R	I	IEC	BN
41077	0A			IEC	NL
41078	0E			IEC	NL
41079	0A	R	I	IEC	NL
41080	0E	R	I	IEC	NL
41081	0A	R	I	IEC	BN
41082	0E	R	I	IEC	BN
41083	0A	R	I	IEC	BN
41084	0E	R	I	IEC	BN
41085	0A	R	I	IEC	BN
41086	0E	R	I	IEC	BN
41087	0A	R	I	IEC	BN
41088	0E	R	I	IEC	BN
41089	0A	R	I	IEC	BN
41090	0E	R	I	IEC	BN
41091	0A	R	I	IEC	BN
41092	0E	R	I	IEC	BN
41093	0A	R	I	IEC	BN
41094	0E	R	I	IEC	BN
41095	0A	R	I	IEC	BN
41096	0E	R	I	IEC	BN
41097	0A	R	I	IML	NL
41098	0E	R	I	IML	NL
41099	0A	R	I	IEC	NL
41100	0E	R	I	IEC	NL
41101	0A	R	I	IEC	NL
41102	0E	R	I	IEC	NL
41103	0A	R	I	IEC	NL
41104	0E	R	I	IEC	NL
41105	0A	R	I	IEC	NL
41106	0E	R	I	IEC	NL
41107	0A	R	I	IEC	BN
41108	0E	R	I	IEC	BN
41109	0A	R	I	IEC	BN
41110	0E	R	I	IEC	BN
41111	0A	R	I	IEC	HT
41112	0E	R	I	IEC	HT
41113	0A	R	I	IEC	BN
41114	0E			IEC	BN
41115	0A	R	I	IEC	BN
41116	0E	R	I	IEC	BN
41117	0A	R	I	IML	NL
41118	0E	R	I	IEC	BN
41119	0A	R	I	IEC	BN
41120	0E	R	I	IEC	BN
41121	2D	PR	I	IWR	LA
41122	0D	PR	I	IWR	LA
41123	2B	PR	I	IWR	PM
41124	0F	R	I	IWR	PM
41125	0D	R	I	IWR	LA
41126	2D	PR	I	IWR	LA
41127	2B	PR	I	IWR	PM
41128	0F	R	I	IWR	PM
41129	2B	PR	I	IWR	OO
41130	0F	R	I	IWR	OO

Veh No	Dia	SC	Liv	Pool	Dep	Veh No	Dia	SC	Liv	Pool	Dep
41131	2B	PR	I	IWR	00	41154	0F	R	I	IML	NL
41132	0F	PR	I	IWR	00	41155	0B		I	IML	NL
41133	2B	R	I	IWR	00	41156	0F		I	IML	NL
41134	0F	R	I	IWR	00	41157	0B			IML	NL
41135	2B	PR	I	IWR	00	41158	0F			IML	NL
41136	0F	R	I	IWR	00	41159	0B	R	I	ICC	PM
41137	0B	P		IWR	PM	41160	0B	R	I	ICC	PM
41138	0F			IWR	PM	41161	0B			ICC	PM
41139	2B	PR	I	IWR	00	41162	0B	R	I	ICC	LA
41140	0F	R	I	IWR	00	41163	0B	R	I	ICC	LA
41141	2B	PR	I	IWR	LA	41164	0B	R	I	IWR	LA
41142	0F	R	I	IWR	LA	41165	0B	R	I	ICC	LA
41143	2B	PR	I	IWR	00	41166	0B			ICC	LA
41144	0F	R	I	IWR	00	41167	0B			ICC	LA
41145	2B	PR	I	IWR	LA	41168	0B			ICC	LA
41146	0F	R	I	IWR	LA	41169	0B			ICC	LA
41147	0B	R	I	ICC	PM	41170	1C	R	I	IEC	BN
41148	0B	R	I	ICC	PM	41171	1C	R	I	IEC	BN
41149	0F	R	I	IEC	BN	41172	1G	R	I	IEC	BN
41150	0F	R	I	IEC	BN	41173	1G	R	I	IEC	BN
41151	0B	PR	I	IEC	BN	41174	1C	R	I	IEC	BN
41152	0F	PR	I	IEC	BN	41175	0B			IML	NL
41153	0B	R	I	IML	NL	41176	0A			IML	NL

TS: Trailer Standard

Diagram	Weight	Seats	Bogies	Variation
GH2.02.0B	34 tonnes	72	BT10	
GH2.02.0D	35 tonnes	72	BT10	All non-smoking
GH2.02.0E	34 tonnes	72	BT10	All non-smoking
GH2.02.0G	35 tonnes	72	BT10	
GH2.02.0H	34 tonnes	72	BT10	
GH2.02.0J	33.5 tonnes	72	BT10b	
GH2.03.0D	33.5 tonnes	76★	BT10b	Refurbished, non-smoking*
GH2.03.0E	33.5 tonnes	76★	BT10b	Refurbished, non-smoking*
GH2.03.0F	33.5 tonnes	76★	BT10d	Non-smoking
GH2.03.0H	34 tonnes	76★	BT10	Non-smoking
GH2.03.0J	33.5 tonnes	76★	BT10b	Refurbished
GH2.03.0K	34 tonnes	76★	BT10	Refurbished
GH2.03.0L	35 tonnes	76★	BT10	Refurbished, non-smoking
GH2.03.0M	33 tonnes	76★	BT10	Refurbished

*No discernible variation
Toilets: 2.

Veh No	Dia	SC	Liv	Pool	Dep	Veh No	Dia	SC	Liv	Pool	Dep
42003	20D	R★	I	IWR	PM	42049	20E	R	I	IWR	LA
42004	20D	R★	I	IWR	PM	42050	20H	R	I	IWR	LA
42005	20G	R★	I	IWR	PM	42051	20E	R	I	IWR	OO
42006	20D	R	I	IWR	PM	42052	20E	R	I	IWR	OO
42007	20D	R	I	IWR	PM	42053	20H	R	I	IWR	OO
42008	20G	R	I	IWR	PM	42054	20E	R	I	IWR	OO
42009	20D	R★	I	IWR	PM	42055	20E	R	I	IWR	OO
42010	20D	R★	I	IWR	PM	42056	20H	R	I	IWR	OO
42011	20G	R★	I	IWR	PM	42057	20E			IML	NL
42012	20D	R★	I	IWR	PM	42058	20E			IML	NL
42013	20D	R★	I	IWR	PM	42059	20H			IML	NL
42014	20G	R★	I	IWR	PM	42060	20E	R	I	IWR	LA
42015	20D	R	I	IWR	PM	42061	20H	R	I	IWR	LA
42016	20D	R	I	IWR	PM	42062	20E	R	I	IML	NL
42017	20G	R	I	IWR	PM	42063	20E	R	I	IML	NL
42018	20D			IWR	PM	42064	20E	R	I	IML	NL
42019	20D			IWR	PM	42065	20H	R	I	IML	NL
42020	20G			IWR	PM	42066	20E	R	I	IML	NL
42021	20D	R	I	IWR	PM	42067	20E	R	I	IML	NL
42022	20D	R	I	IWR	PM	42068	20H	R	I	IML	NL
42023	20H	R	I	IWR	PM	42069	20E			IML	NL
42024	20E	R	I	IWR	PM	42070	20E			IML	NL
42025	20E	R	I	IWR	PM	42071	20E			IML	NL
42026	20H	R	I	IWR	PM	42072	20E	R	I	IML	NL
42027	20E			IWR	PM	42073	20E	R	I	IML	NL
42028	20E			IWR	PM	42074	20H	R	I	IML	NL
42029	20E			IWR	PM	42075	20H	R★	I	IML	NL
42030	20E			IWR	PM	42076	20E	R	I	IML	NL
42031	20E			IWR	PM	42077	20E	R	I	IML	NL
42032	20H			IWR	PM	42078	20H	R★	I	IML	NL
42033	20E	R	I	IWR	LA	42079	20E			IML	NL
42034	20E	R	I	IWR	LA	42080	20H			IML	NL
42035	20H	R	I	IWR	LA	42081	20E	R	I	IML	NL
42036	20E	R	I	IWR	LA	42082	20E	R	I	IML	NL
42037	20D	R	I	IWR	LA	42083	20E	R	I	IML	NL
42038	20H	R	I	IWR	LA	42084	20E			ICC	PM
42039	20E	R	I	IWR	LA	42085	20E			ICC	PM
42040	20E	R	I	IWR	LA	42086	20E			ICC	PM
42041	20H	R	I	IWR	LA	42087	20H			ICC	PM
42042	20E	R	I	IWR	LA	42088	20E	R	I	ICC	LA
42043	20E	R	I	IWR	LA	42089	20E	R	I	ICC	LA
42044	20H	R	I	IWR	LA	42090	20E	R	I	ICC	LA
42045	20E	R★	I	IWR	LA	42091	20H	R	I	ICC	LA
42046	20E	R★	I	IWR	LA	42092	20E	R	I	ICC	LA
42047	20H	R★	I	IWR	LA	42093	20E	R	I	ICC	LA
42048	20E	R	I	IWR	LA	42094	20E	R	I	ICC	LA
						42095	20H	R	I	ICC	LA

Veh No	Dia	SC	Liv	Pool	Dep	Veh No	Dia	SC	Liv	Pool	Dep
42096	20E	R	I	IWR	LA	42145	20H			IEC	NL
42097	20E	R	I	IWR	LA	42146	20E	★	I	IML	NL
42098	20E	R	I	IWR	LA	42147	30H	R★	I	IEC	BN
42099	20E	R	I	IWR	LA	42148	30H	R★	I	IEC	BN
42100	20K	R★	I	IEC	NL	42149	30K	R★	I	IEC	BN
42101	20K	R★	I	IEC	BN	42150	20E	★	I	IML	NL
42102	30K	R★	I	IEC	BN	42151	20E			IEC	NL
42103	20E	R★	I	IEC	BN	42152	20E			IEC	NL
42104	20E	R★	I	IEC	BN	42153	20H			IEC	NL
42105	20H	R★	I	IEC	BN	42154	20E	★	I	IML	NL
42106	20H	R★	I	IEC	BN	42155	30H	R★	I	IEC	NL
42107	20H	R★	I	IEC	BN	42156	30H	R★	I	IEC	NL
42108	20E	R	I	ICC	LA	42157	30H	R★	I	IEC	NL
42109	20E	R	I	ICC	LA	42158	30D	★	I	IML	NL
42110	20E	R	I	ICC	LA	42159	30H	R★	I	IEC	BN
42111	20E	R	I	IEC	BN	42160	30H	R★	I	IEC	BN
42112	20E	R	I	IEC	BN	42161	30H	R★	I	IEC	BN
42113	20H	R	I	IEC	BN	42162	20E	R★	I	IEC	BN
42115	20E	R	I	IEC	BN	42163	30H	R★	I	IEC	BN
42116	20H	R	I	IEC	BN	42164	20H	R★	I	IEC	BN
42117	20E	R	I	IEC	BN	42165	20H	R★	I	IEC	BN
42118	20H			IML	NL	42166	20E	R★	I	IEC	BN
42119	20E	R	I	IEC	BN	42167	20E	R★	I	IEC	BN
42120	20E	R	I	IEC	BN	42168	20E	R★	I	IEC	BN
42121	20H	R	I	IEC	BN	42169	20E	R★	I	IEC	BN
42122	20H	R★	I	IEC	BN	42170	20E	R★	I	IEC	BN
42123	20H	R★	I	IEC	BN	42171	20E	R★	I	IEC	BN
42124	20E	R★	I	IEC	BN	42172	20E	R★	I	IEC	BN
42125	30K	R★	I	IEC	BN	42173	20H	R★	I	IEC	BN
42126	20H	R	I	IML	NL	42174	20H	R★	I	IEC	BN
42127	20E	R	I	IEC	BN	42175	20E	R★	I	IEC	BN
42128	20H	R	I	IEC	BN	42176	20E	R★	I	IEC	BN
42129	20B			IEC	BN	42177	20E	R★	I	IEC	BN
42130	20E	R★	I	IEC	BN	42178	30H	R★	I	IEC	BN
42131	20E	R★	I	IEC	NL	42179	20E	R	I	IEC	BN
42132	20E	R★	I	IEC	NL	42180	20E	R	I	IEC	BN
42133	20H	R★	I	IEC	NL	42181	20E	R	I	IEC	BN
42134	20E	R★	I	IEC	BN	42182	20E	R★	I	IEC	BN
42135	20E	R★	I	IEC	NL	42183	20E	R★	I	IEC	BN
42136	20E	R★	I	IEC	NL	42184	20E	R★	I	IEC	BN
42137	20H	R★	I	IEC	NL	42185	20E	R★	I	IEC	BN
42138	20E	R★	I	IEC	BN	42186	20E	R★	I	IEC	BN
42139	30H	R★	I	IEC	NL	42187	20E	R★	I	IEC	BN
42140	30H	R★	I	IEC	NL	42188	20E	R★	I	IEC	BN
42141	30K	R★	I	IEC	NL	42189	20H	R★	I	IEC	BN
42143	20E			IEC	NL	42190	20E	R★	I	IEC	BN
42144	20E			IEC	NL	42191	20E	R★	I	IML	NL

Veh No	Dia	SC	Liv	Pool	Dep	Veh No	Dia	SC	Liv	Pool	Dep
42192	20E	R★	I	IML	NL	42239	20H	R★	I	IEC	BN
42193	20H	R★	I	IML	NL	42240	20E		I	IML	NL
42194	20B	R★	I	IEC	BN	42241	20E	R★	I	IEC	BN
42195	20E	R★	I	IML	NL	42242	20E	R★	I	IEC	BN
42196	20E	R★	I	IWR	LA	42243	20E	R	I	IEC	BN
42197	20E	R★	I	IWR	LA	42244	20H	R	I	IEC	BN
42198	20B	R★	I	IEC	NL	42245	20E			IML	NL
42199	20H	R★	I	IEC	NL	42246	20E	R★	I	IEC	BN
42200	20E	R★	I	IML	NL	42247	20E	R★	I	IEC	BN
42201	20E	R★	I	IEC	NL	42248	20E	R★	I	IEC	BN
42202	20E	R★	I	IEC	NL	42249	20H	R★	I	IEC	BN
42203	20E	R★	I	IEC	NL	42250	20H			IML	NL
42204	20H	R★	I	IEC	NL	42251	30E	R★	I	IWR	LA
42205	20E	R★	I	IML	NL	42252	30D	R★	I	IWR	LA
42206	20E	R★	I	IEC	NL	42253	30J	R★	I	IWR	LA
42207	20E	R★	I	IEC	NL	42254	20F	R★	I	ICC	PM
42208	20E	R★	I	IEC	NL	42255	20F	R★	I	IWR	PM
42209	20H	R★	I	IEC	NL	42256	20F	R★	I	IWR	PM
42210	20H	R★	I	IML	NL	42257	20J	R★	I	IWR	PM
42211	20E	R★	I	IEC	NL	42258	20F	R★	I	ICC	PM
42212	20E	R★	I	IEC	NL	42259	30D	R★	I	IWR	LA
42213	20E	R★	I	IEC	NL	42260	30D	R★	I	IWR	LA
42214	20H	R★	I	IEC	NL	42261	30J	R★	I	IWR	LA
42215	20E	R★	I	IML	NL	42262	20F	R★	I	ICC	PM
42216	30H	R★	I	IWR	LA	42263	20F	R★	I	IWR	PM
42217	20E	R★	I	IEC	BN	42264	20F	R★	I	IWR	PM
42218	20E	R★	I	IEC	BN	42265	20J	R★	I	IWR	PM
42219	20H	R★	I	IEC	BN	42266	20J	R★	I	ICC	PM
42220	20E	R★	I	IML	NL	42267	20F	R★	I	IWR	00
42221	30H	R★	I	IWR	LA	42268	20F	R★	I	IWR	00
42222	20E	R	I	IEC	BN	42269	20J	R★	I	IWR	00
42223	20E	R	I	IEC	BN	42270	20F	R★	I	ICC	PM
42224	20H	R	I	IEC	BN	42271	20F	R★	I	IWR	00
42225	20E	R★	I	IML	NL	42272	20F	R★	I	IWR	00
42226	20E	R★	I	IEC	BN	42273	20J	R★	I	IWR	00
42227	20E	R★	I	IEC	HT	42274	20F	R★	I	ICC	PM
42228	20E	R★	I	IEC	HT	42275	20F	R★	I	IWR	00
42229	20H	R★	I	IEC	NL	42276	20F	R★	I	IWR	00
42230	20H	R★	I	IML	NL	42277	20J	R★	I	IWR	00
42231	20B	R★	I	IEC	BN	42278	20F	R★	I	ICC	PM
42232	20E			IEC	BN	42279	30D	R★	I	IWR	00
42233	20E			IEC	BN	42280	30D	R★	I	IWR	00
42234	20H			IEC	BN	42281	30J	R★	I	IWR	00
42235	20E			IML	NL	42282	20J	R	I	ICC	PM
42236	20E			IML	NL	42283	20F			IWR	PM
42237	20E	R★	I	IEC	BN	42284	20F			IWR	PM
42238	20E	R★	I	IEC	BN	42285	20J			IWR	PM

Veh No	Dia	SC	Liv	Pool	Dep	Veh No	Dia	SC	Liv	Pool	Dep
42286	20F	R	I	ICC	PM	42316	20F			ICC	LA
42287	20F	R★	I	IWR	OO	42317	20J			ICC	LA
42288	20F	R★	I	IWR	OO	42318	20F			ICC	LA
42289	20J	R★	I	IWR	OO	42319	20F			ICC	LA
42290	20F	R★	I	ICC	PM	42320	20F			ICC	LA
42291	20F	R★	I	IWR	LA	42321	20J			ICC	LA
42292	20F	R★	I	IWR	LA	42322	20J	R	I	ICC	LA
42293	20J	R★	I	IWR	LA	42323	30F	★		IML	NL
42294	20F	R	I	ICC	PM	42324	30F	★		IEC	NL
42295	20F	R★	I	IWR	OO	42325	30F	R★	I	IML	NL
42296	20F	R★	I	IWR	OO	42326	30F	R★	I	IEC	BN
42297	20J	R★	I	IWR	OO	42327	30F	R★	I	IEC	BN
42298	20F	R	I	ICC	PM	42328	30F	R★	I	IEC	BN
42299	20F	R★	I	IWR	LA	42329	30F	R★	I	IEC	NL
42300	20F	R★	I	IWR	LA	42330	30F	R★	I	IEC	BN
42301	20J	R★	I	IWR	LA	42331	30F	R★	I	IEC	NL
42302	20F	R	I	ICC	PM	42332	30F	★		IML	NL
42303	20F	R	I	ICC	PM	42333	30F	★		IEC	NL
42304	20F	R	I	ICC	PM	42334	30F	R★	I	IEC	BN
42305	20J	R	I	ICC	PM	42335	30F	R★	I	IEC	BN
42306	20F			ICC	LA	42336	30F	R★	I	IEC	BN
42307	20F			ICC	LA	42337	30F	R★	I	IEC	BN
42308	20F			ICC	LA	42338	30F	R★	I	IEC	BN
42309	20J			ICC	LA	42339	30F	★		IEC	NL
42310	20F			ICC	LA	42340	30F	R★	I	IML	NL
42311	20F			ICC	LA	42341	30D	★		IEC	BN
42312	20F			ICC	LA	42342	30D	R★	I	IWR	LA
42313	20J			ICC	LA	42343	30D	R★	I	IWR	LA
42314	20F			ICC	LA	42344	30D	R★	I	IWR	LA
42315	20F			ICC	LA	42345	30D	R★	I	IWR	LA

TGS: Trailer Guard Standard

Diagram	Weight	Variation
GJ2.01.0A	33.5 tonnes	
GJ2.01.0B	34 tonnes	Additional standard coupling and buffers for ac electric locomotive haulage

Bogies: BT10b   **Seats:** 63
Equipment: Public address transmitter   **Toilets:** 1.

Veh No	Dia	SC	Liv	Pool	Dep	Veh No	Dia	SC	Liv	Pool	Dep
44000	0A	R	I	ICC	PM	44003	0A	R	I	IWR	PM
44001	0A	R	I	IWR	PM	44004	0A	R	I	IWR	PM
44002	0A	R	I	IWR	PM	44005	0A	R	I	IWR	PM

Veh No	Dia	SC	Liv	Pool	Dep	Veh No	Dia	SC	Liv	Pool	Dep
44006	0A			IWR	PM	44052	0A	R	I	IEC	NL
44007	0A	R	I	IWR	PM	44053	0A	R	I	IEC	BN
44008	0A	R	I	IWR	PM	44054	0A	R	I	IEC	BN
44009	0A			IWR	PM	44055	0A	R	I	IEC	BN
44010	0A			IWR	PM	44056	0B	R	I	IEC	BN
44011	0A	R	I	IWR	LA	44057	0A	R	I	IEC	BN
44012	0A	R	I	IWR	LA	44058	0A	R	I	IEC	BN
44013	0A	R	I	IWR	LA	44059	0B	R	I	IEC	BN
44014	0A	R	I	IWR	LA	44060	0A	R	I	IEC	BN
44015	0A	R	I	IWR	LA	44061	0A	R	I	IML	NL
44016	0A	R	I	IWR	LA	44062	0A	R	I	ICC	PM
44017	0A	R	I	IWR	00	44063	0A	R	I	IEC	NL
44018	0A	R	I	IWR	00	44064	0A	R	I	IEC	NL
44019	0A			IWR	NL	44065	0A	R	I	ICC	PM
44020	0A	R	I	IWR	LA	44066	0A	R	I	IEC	NL
44021	0A	R	I	IML	NL	44067	0A	R	I	IEC	NL
44022	0A	R	I	IML	NL	44068	0A	R	I	ICC	PM
44023	0A			IML	NL	44069	0A			ICC	PM
44024	0A	R	I	IML	NL	44070	0A	R	I	IEC	BN
44025	0A	R	I	IML	NL	44071	0A	R	I	IEC	BN
44026	0A			IML	NL	44072	0A	R	I	ICC	LA
44027	0A	R	I	IML	NL	44073	0A	R	I	IEC	HT
44028	0A	R	I	IWR	LA	44074	0A			IEC	BN
44029	0A	R	I	IWR	PM	44075	0A	R	I	IEC	BN
44030	0A	R	I	IWR	LA	44076	0A	R	I	ICC	LA
44031	0A	R	I	IWR	PM	44077	0A	R	I	IEC	BN
44032	0A	R	I	IWR	00	44078	0A	R	I	IEC	BN
44033	0A	R	I	IWR	00	44079	0A	R	I	IEC	BN
44034	0A	R	I	IWR	00	44080	0A	R	I	IEC	BN
44035	0A	R	I	IWR	00	44081	0A	R	I	IWR	PM
44036	0A			IWR	PM	44083	0A	R	I	IML	NL
44037	0A	R	I	IWR	00	44084	0A	R	I	ICC	LA
44038	0A	R	I	IWR	LA	44085	0A	R	I	IML	NL
44039	0A	R	I	IWR	00	44086	0B			IML	NL
44040	0A	R	I	IWR	LA	44087	0A	R	I	ICC	LA
44041	0A	R	I	IEC	BN	44088	0A			ICC	LA
44042	0A	R	I	IEC	BN	44089	0A			ICC	LA
44043	0A	R	I	IEC	BN	44090	0A			ICC	LA
44044	0A	R	I	IEC	BN	44091	0A			ICC	LA
44045	0A	R	I	IEC	BN	44093	0A	R	I	IEC	BN
44046	0A	R	I	IEC	NL	44094	0A			IML	NL
44047	0A		I	IEC	NL	44097	0A	R		IEC	HT
44048	0A	R	I	IEC	NL	44098	0B	R		IEC	BN
44049	0A			IEC	NL	44099	0A	R	I	IWR	00
44050	0A	R	I	IEC	BN	44100	0A			IML	NL
44051	0A			IEC	NL	44101	0B			IEC	BN

IC125 TRAILER CAR FORMATIONS

CLASS 253 WESTERN REGION

Unit		Allocation		GH1	GH1	GN4	GH2	GH2	GH2	GJ2
01	R	IWR	PM	41003	41004	40209	42003	42004	42005	44001
02	R	IWR	PM	41005	41006	40212	42006	42007	42008	44002
03	R	IWR	PM	41007	41008	40213	42009	42010	42011	44003
04	R	IWR	PM	41009	41010	40204	42012	42013	42014	44004
05	R	IWR	PM	41011	41012	40205	42015	42016	42017	44005
06		IWR	PM	41013	41014	40206	42018	42019	42020	44006
07	R	IWR	PM	41015	41016	40207	42021	42022	42023	44007
08	R	IWR	PM	41017	41018	40208	42024	42025	42026	44008
09		IWR	PM	41019	41020	40211	42027	42028	42029	44009
10		IWR	PM	41021	41022	40210	42030	42031	42032	44010

Unit		Allocation		GH1	GH1	GK1† GK2*/GK4	GH2	GH2	GH2	GH2	GJ2
11	R	IWR	LA	41023	41024	40355	42096	42033	42034	42035	44011
12	R	IWR	LA	41025	41026	40323	42097	42036	42037	42038	44012
13	R	IWR	LA	41027	41028	40325	42098	42039	42040	42041	44013
14	R	IWR	LA	41029	41030	40326	42099	42042	42043	42044	44014
15	R	IWR	LA	41031	41032	40327	42216	42045	42046	42047	44015
16	R	IWR	LA	41033	41034	40331	42221	42048	42049	42050	44016
17	R	IWR	OO	41035	41036	40417*	—	42051	42052	42053	44017
18	R	IWR	OO	41037	41038	40419*	—	42054	42055	42056	44018
28	P	IWR	LA	41121	41122	40322	42345	42251	42252	42253	44028
29	R	IWR	PM	41123	41124	40422*	—	42255	42256	42257	44029
30	R	IWR	LA	41126	41125	40324	42344	42259	42260	42261	44030
31	R	IWR	PM	41127	41128	40435*	—	42263	42264	42265	44031
32	R	IWR	OO	41129	41130	40436*	—	42267	42268	42269	44032
33	R	IWR	OO	41131	41132	40437*	—	42271	42272	42273	44033
34	R	IWR	OO	41133	41134	40427*	—	42275	42276	42277	44034
35	R	IWR	OO	41135	41136	40423*	—	42279	42280	42281	44035
36		IWR	PM	41137	41138	40428*	—	42283	42284	42285	44036
37	R	IWR	OO	41139	41140	40416*	—	42287	42288	42289	44037
38	P	IWR	LA	41141	41142	40732†	42342	42291	42292	42293	44038
39	R	IWR	OO	41143	41144	40418*	—	42295	42296	42297	44039
40	P	IWR	LA	41145	41146	40757†	42343	42299	42300	42301	44040
41	R	ICC	PM	—	41147	40401*	42254	42258	42262	42266	44000
42	R	ICC	PM	—	41148	40402*	42270	42274	42278	42282	44062
43	R	ICC	PM	—	41159	40403*	42286	42290	42294	42298	44065
44	R	ICC	PM	—	41160	40425*	42302	42303	42304	42305	44068
45		ICC	PM	—	41161	40421*	42084	42085	42086	42087	44069
46	R	ICC	LA	—	41162	40414*	42088	42089	42090	42091	44072

Unit		Allocation		GH1	GH1	GK1† GK2*/GK4	GH2	GH2	GH2	GH2	GJ2
47	R	ICC	LA	—	41163	40415*	42092	42093	42094	42095	44076
50	R	ICC	LA	—	41042	40424*	42196	42197	42060	42061	44020
51	R	ICC	LA	—	41165	40430*	42108	42109	42110	42322	44087
52		ICC	LA	—	41166	40431*	42306	42307	42308	42309	44088
53		ICC	LA	—	41167	40432*	42310	42311	42312	42313	44089
54		ICC	LA	—	41168	40433*	42314	42315	42316	42317	44090
55		ICC	LA	—	41169	40434*	42318	42319	42320	42321	44091

Spare coaches GK2: (R) 40420, 40426.

GH1: (R) 41164.

GJ2: (R) 44081, 44084, 44099.

Refurbished set/vehicle: R; Refurbished for Pullman service: P.

CLASS 254 EAST COAST & MIDLAND MAIN LINES

Unit		Allocation		GH1	GH1/ GH2*	GH1†/GK1 GH2‡/GL1*	GH1/GH2† GK1*	GH2/ GK1*	GH2	GH2	GH2	GJ2
01	R	IEC	BN	41057	41058	40708	—	42335	42111	42112	42113	44041
02	R	IEC	BN	41059	41060	40733	—	42336	42115	42116	42117	44042
03	R	IEC	BN	41061	41062	40729	—	42337	42119	42120	42121	44043
04	R	IEC	BN	41063	41064	40754	—	42328	42123	42124	42125	44044
05	R	IEC	BN	41171	41173	40734	—	42338	42178	42127	42128	44045
06	R	IEC	NL	41067	41068	40749	—	42331	42131	42132	42133	44046
07	R	IEC	NL	41069	41070	40751	—	42339	42135	42136	42137	44047
08	R	IEC	NL	41071	41072	40728	—	42329	42139	42140	42141	44048
09		IEC	NL	41073	41074	40752	—	42333	42143	42144	42145	44049
10	R	IEC	BN	41075	41076	40756	—	42327	42147	42148	42149	44050
11		IEC	NL	41077	41078	40753	—	42324	42151	42152	42153	44051
12	R	IEC	NL	41079	41080	40700	—	42155	42156	42157	42100	44052
13	R	IEC	BN	41081	41082	40701	—	42159	42160	42161	42101	44053
14	R	IEC	BN	41083	41084	40702	—	42163	42164	42165	42102	44054
15	R	IEC	BN	41085	41086	40703	—	42169	42168	42167	42103	44055
16	R	IEC	BN	41087	41088	40706	—	42104	42171	42172	42173	44056
17	R	IEC	BN	41089	41090	40705	—	42175	42176	42177	42105	44057
18	R	IEC	BN	41091	41092	40704	—	42179	42180	42181	42106	44058
19	R	IEC	BN	41093	41094	40707	—	42183	42184	42185	42107	44059
20	R	IEC	BN	41095	41096	40736	—	42326	42187	42188	42189	44060
21	P	IML	NL	41097	41098	41117†	40619§*	42191	42192	42193	—	44061
22	P	IEC	NL	41099	41041	40501*	41100	40711*	42198	42199	—	44063
23	R	IEC	NL	41101	41102	40712	—	42201	42202	42203	42204	44064
24	R	IEC	NL	41103	41104	40713	—	42206	42207	42208	42209	44066
25	R	IEC	NL	41105	41106	40714	—	42211	42212	42213	42214	44067
26	P	IEC	BN	41113	41108	41107†	40715*	—	42217	42218	42219	44070
27	R	IEC	BN	41109	41110	40716	—	42334	42222	42223	42224	44071

Unit		Allocation	GH1	GH1/ GH2*	GH1†/GK1 GH2‡/GL1*	GH1/GH2† GK1*	GH2/ GK1*	GH2	GH2	GH2	GJ2
28	P	IEC HT	41112	41066	40511*	41111	40730*	42227	42228	—	44073
29		IEC BN	41114	42194*	42231*	42341†	40718*	42232	42233	42234	44098+
30	R	IEC BN	41115	41116	40710	—	42330	42237	42238	42239	44075
31	R	IEC BN	41170	41118	40720	—	42241	42242	42243	42244	44077
32	R	IEC BN	41119	41120	40721	—	42246	42247	42248	42249	44078
33	R	IEC BN	41149	41150	40739	—	42226	42182	42186	42190	44079
34	R	IEC BN	41151	41152	40740	—	42226	42182	42186	42190	44080
35	R	IML NL	41153	41154	40741	—	42195	42200	42205	42210	44083
36	R	IML NL	41155	41156	40748	—	42215	42220	42225	42230	44085
37		IML NL	41157	41158	40743	—	42235	42240	42245	42250	44086
38	R	IML NL	41055	41056	40709	—	42081	42082	42083	42126	44027
39	R	IML NL	41045	41065	40738	—	42062	42066	42067	42068	44022
40		IML NL	41047	41048	40744	—	42069	42070	42071	42118	44023
41	R	IML NL	41049	41050	40745	—	42325	42072	42073	42074	44024
42	R	IML NL	41051	41052	40746	—	42075	42076	42077	42078	44025
43		IML NL	41053	41054	40747	—	42332	42236	42079	42080	44026
44	R	IEC BN	41174	41172	40742	—	42130	42134	42138	42122	44093
45		IML NL	41176	41175	40750	—	42158	42146	42150	42154	44094
46		IML NL	41039	41040	40735	—	42323	42057	42058	42059	44019
47	R	IML NL	41044	41043	40737	—	42340	42063	42064	42065	44021

§Modular catering

Spare coaches *GL1:* (P) 40505.
        GM4: 40513 (for private hire).
        GK2: (R) 40429.
        GK1: (R) 40717, 40739.
        GH1: (R) 41044, 41046.
        GH2: 42129, (R) 42229.
        GJ2: (R) 44097. 44074, 44100, 44101.
        +Peterborough set. Buffer fitted GJ2 temporarily in place of No 44074.
        Refurbished set/vehicle: R; Refurbished for Pullman service: P.

Service Department Special Purpose Vehicles

Class 97/2	Type 2	A1A-A1A

Former Class 31/1 locomotives. Details as Capital Stock Diagram 31-1CX.

Diagram: 97-2DX
Sector: *Departmental:* **DRTC:** Research
Livery: Research Red, white and black

Loco No	Dia	SC		Pool	Dep
97204	DX	K		DRTC	HQ

Note: Former No 31326

Class 97/2	ETHEL	2-2

Electric Train Heating Mobile Generators
Former Class 25/3 locomotives. Not self-propelled.

Built: British Railways Derby 1966, converted at Aberdeen Ferryhill TMD, 1983
Engine: Sulzer 6LDA28B, 6-cyl, 4-stroke of 1,250hp
Dimensions: 50.5ft L × 9ft W × 12.7ft H
Weight: 63 tonnes
Main generator: AEI RTB 15656
ETH Index: 54
Route availability: 5

Fuel: 500gal
Train brake: Dual air and vacuum
Maximum operating speed: 75mph
Diagram: 97-2BX

Sector: *InterCity:* **ICHA:** Charter
Livery: InterCity

Loco No	Dia	Pool	Dep	Name
97251	BX	ICHA	CL	Ethel 2
97252	BX	ICHA	OC	Ethel 3

Class 97/4	Type 4	1CO-CO1

Former Class 46 locomotives.

Built: British Railways, Derby 1962
Engine: Sulzer 12LDA28B, 12-cyl, 4-stroke of 2,500hp
Dimensions: 67.9ft L × 9.1ft W × 12.8ft H
Weight: 140 tonnes
Power/Control equipment: Six Brush TM73-68 Mk III traction motors, main generator Brush TG160-60
Route availability: 7
Fuel: 790gal
Train brake: Dual air and vacuum
Brake force: 63 tonnes
Maximum tractive effort: 55,000lb

Maximum operating speed: 90mph
Train heating: Steam generator, Spanner Swirlyflow Mk III, 1,850lb/hr (isolated)
Water tanks: 1,040gal
Diagram: 97-4AX

Sector: *Departmental:* **DRTC:** Research
Special livery: Research Red and blue: 97403

Loco No	Dia	Pool	Dep		Name
97403	AX	DRTC	HQ		Ixion
97404	AX	DRTC	HQ	(Su Egginton Jct) (for spare equipment only)	

Class 97/4	Type 4	CO-CO

Former Capital Stock Class 47/4.

Built: British Railways 1964

New Diagram	Equivalent Diagram
97-4BX	47-4HX
97-4CX	47-4KX

Maximum speed: 100mph

Sector: *Departmental:* **DRTC:** Research
(NB: Usage on non-RTC duties subject to special DMEE authority.)

Loco No	Former No	Dia	SC	Pool	Dep
97472	(47472)	BX	B	DRTC	CD
97480	(47480)	BX		DRTC	CD
	Robin Hood				
97545	(47545)	BX		DRTC	CD
97561	(47561)	CX	B	DRTC	CD

Class 97/0	Shunters	0-6-0

Diagram 97-OAO
Built: Ruston and Hornsby 1959
Engine: Ruston Mk 6 VPHL, 6-cyl, 4-stroke of 165hp
Dimensions: 25ft L × 8.5ft W × 11ft H
Weight: 30.7 tonnes
Power/Control equipment: BTH traction motor RTA 5041, main generator BTH RTB 6034
Route availability: 1
Maximum tractive effort: 17,000lb
Fuel: 80gal
Maximum operating speed: 20mph
Train brakes: Not equipped
Brake force: 16 tonnes

Sector: *Departmental:* **DCSA**: DCE, Western Region

Diagram 97-ODA
Former Capital Stock Class 08. For details see Diagram 08-OFA
Built: British Railways, Derby, 1959

Sector: *Network SouthEast:* **NXXA**: General, Shunters
Livery: Network SouthEast

Diagram 97-OEV
Former Capital Stock Class 03.
Built: British Railways, Doncaster, 1959
Train brake: Vacuum only

Sector: *Departmental:* **DCSA**: DCE, Southern Region

Diagram 97-OFX
Former Capital Stock Class 09. For details see Diagram 09-OAX
Built: British Railways, Horwich, 1961

Sector: *Departmental:* **DCWA**: DCE Western Region
Livery: Blue, grey cab sides

Loco No	Dia	Pool	Dep	Name
97651	AO	DCWA	CF (@ GL)	
97653	AO	DCWA	CF (@ RR)	
97654	AO	DCWA	RG	
97800	DA	NXXA	SG	Ivor
97805	EV	DCSA	RY	
97806	FX	DCWA	CF (@ Sudbrook)	

Class 97/7	Battery Electric	B0-B0

Built: 1974-80 from British Railways 1957 built Class 501 DMBS vehicles
Supply: Third rail 750V dc and 320V dc batteries
Dimensions: 60.6ft L × 8ft W × 11.6ft H
Weight: 58.9 tonnes
Power/Control equipment: Four GEC WT344A 185hp traction motors, drive spur gear and pinion, compressor GEC DH28
Locomotive brake: Electro-pneumatic and Westinghouse automatic
Brake force: 45 tonnes
Maximum operating speed: 25mph
Route availability: 4
Design code: 97-7AE

Standard equipment: Single cab, Multiple working within type (operated in consecutively numbered pairs)
Sector: *Departmental:* **DCEA**: DCE Eastern Region. **DCMA**: DCE Midland

Loco No	Dia	Liv	Pool	Dep
97701	AE		DCMA	HQ (@ BD)
97702	AE		DCMA	HQ (@ BD)
97703	AE		DCEA	HQ (@ HE)
97704	AE		DCEA	HQ (@ HE)
97705	AE		DCEA	HQ (@ HE)
97706	AE		DCEA	HQ (@ HE)
97707	AE	N	DCEA	HQ (@ HE)
97708	AE	N	DCEA	HQ (@ HE)

Special Purpose Locomotives

The following locomotives have been withdrawn from operating stock but are retained for special uses.

ZZB	Mobile Load Bank	2-2

Non-self-propelled mobile load bank used for checking 25kV overhead electric wiring after installation before cleared for normal operating stock tests.

Built: North British Loco Co 1960 as Class 84 25kV ac electric locomotive. Converted to DMEE, RTC, Derby
Dimensions: 53.5ft L × 8.7ft W × 13ft H (pantograph housed)

Equipment: Four GEC WT501 traction motors
Sector: *Departmental:* **DRTC:** Research

No	Pool	Dep
ADB 968021	DRTC	HQ

ZZR	Traction Training	1CO-CO1* or B0-B0

The following locomotives have been retained by depots for artisan training. They are not now self-propelled and may not now be in complete condition. Departmental numbers allocated may not have been applied, therefore last running numbers are also given here.

No	Former No	Former class	Dep	No	Former No	Former class	Dep
ADB 968024	45017	45/0*	TO	ADB 968027	25912	25/9	HO
ADB 968026	25908	25/9	TO	ADB 968028	27024	27/0	ED

LOCOMOTIVE COSTING CENTRES/POOLS/ SUB-SECTORS

The following listings show the *Sector* and *sub-Sector* locomotive Pools corrected to the time of going to press (early February). Although locomotives are allocated to a Traction Maintenance Depot this is solely for the larger repairs and examinations. Operation is now dictated by the Sectors to which locomotives are dedicated. In theory, and increasingly in practice, traction is booked to diagrams which are at least primarily financed by the appropriate sub-Sector and only in emergency situations are they used on other duties. At weekends the passenger Sectors may 'hire' locomotives from other Sectors to cover summer relief work or diversionary services.

Diesel shunters are also now generally funded in a similar manner, but for obvious reasons maintenance has to be less centralised. Thus it is now general practice to allocate the locomotives to a main depot in an Area capable of handling all maintenance whilst they operate, fuel and receive light attention at various Servicing Depots nearer their normal point of duty. *Motive Power Monthly* will continue to provide an updating service for this information as locomotive 'ownership' changes occur and alterations are made to locomotive codes.

CBRE: BREL '88, Shunters (unofficial code)

08168	08470

CHUB: Hunslet-Barclay hire locomotives (unofficial code)

20041	20060	20083	20101	20209	20219	20224	20225

CRFS: RFS Engineering (unofficial code)

08331

CSLA: Steam locomotives, BRHQ

98238	98240	98243						
98372								
98400	98406	98427	98455	98469	98472	98479	98480	98482	98488
98500	98505	98507	98512	98519	98525	98526	98529	98530	98532
98560	98565	98567	98571	98577	98598			
98605	98641	98642	98690	98693	98696			
98700	98701	98709	98715	98727	98729	98750	98751	98771	98780
98792								
98800	98801	98802	98805	98809	98822	98824	98828	98829	98832
98833	98851	98857	98868	98872	98898			
98920								

CYPO: Foster Yeoman, Private owner, Class 59, BRHQ

59001	59002	59003	59004	59005

DBMS: Departmental, BRML

08484	08629	08642	08647	08883	08892

DCAA: Departmental, RCE Anglia

31127	31165	31173	31181	31186	31187	31190	31191	31219	31224
31231	31250	31263	31268						
37140	37216								
47346	47366								

DCAB: Departmental, RCE Anglia, Shunters

08528	08529	08531	08540	08541	08638	08655	08757	08772	08775
08810	08859	08889							

DCEA: Departmental, RCE Eastern

20030	20064	20096							
31118	31123	31170	31208	31221	31242	31247	31278	31281	31282
31283	31285								
31431	31432	31439	31441	31444	31447	31449	31452	31453	31456
31458	31469								
47329	47331	47332	47344	47348	47352				
47417	47418								
97703	97704	97705	97706	97707	97708				

DCEB: Departmental, RCE Eastern, Shunters

08499	08583	08605	08607	08618	08657	08701	08706	08773	08783
08794	08866	08867	08870	08876	08885	08906	08908	08919	08931

DCHA: Departmental, RCE Scottish Region, Eastfield

26011	26014	26015	26021	26023	26024	26026	26027	26028	26035
26036	26039								
37023	37025	37097	37170	37175	37261	37262			
37402	37414								
47467	47518	47546	47550	47604	47617				

DCHB: Departmental, RCE Scottish Region, RETB, Snowplough, Eastfield.

20114	20127	20138

DCMA: Departmental, RCE Midland Region, Bescot.

20005	20029	20032	20034	20042	20048	20054	20056	20063	20070
20072	20097	20099	20121	20124	20139	20147	20158	20160	21076
20178	20183	20195	20217						
31107	31112	31119	31162	31178	31235	31237	31288	31305	31317
31403	31405	31406	31407	31409	31411	31419	31420	31422	31423
31424	31430	31433	31434	31435	31437	31445	31446	31448	31451
31454	31455	31459	31462	31463	31464	31468			
47003	47018	47053	47118						
47333	47339	47340	47343	47353	46356	46357	47358		
47426	47427	47431	47432	47436	47438	47450	47453		
97701	97702								

DCMB: Departmental, RCE Midland Region, Shunters

08573	08612	08619	08624	08628	08666	08702	08784	08789	08815
08843	08891	08894	08922	08925	08927				

DCQA: Departmental DCE Track Test

31412	31414	31416	31426

DCSA: Departmental, RCE Southern

33002	33004	33006	33013	33015	33023	33026	33030	33065	
33107	33110	33117	33118						
33201	33202								
73101	73103	73105	37107	73108	73109	73110	37111	73114	73117
73118	73119	73126	73128	73129	73131	73132	73133	73135	37138
37139									

DCSB: Departmental, RCE Southern, Shunters

08831	08847								
09003	09004	09005	09009	09011	09014	09019	09021	09026	
99800									

DCWA: Departmental, RCE Western

08011									
37133	37141	37142	37146	37158	37174	37207	37220	37263	37264
37272									
47334	47341								
47463	47484	47513	47540	47623	47628				
50004	50005	50007	50008	50009	50015	50016	50020	50021	50042
50045									
50149									
97651	97653	97654							
97806									

DMEA (ex-DWCQ): Departmental, DMEE Nationwide, BRHQ

20066	20148	20193	20202	20204	20227				
26010	26042	26043	26046						
31101	31105	31106	31131	31135	31196	31205	31206	31230	31232
31252	31255	31260	31264	31272	31286	31289	31290	31392	31323
31413	31415	31417	31457	31460	31461	31465			
33025									
33111									
73136									

DMES (ex-DWCS): Departmental, DMEE Shunters: BRHQ

08393	08411	08417	08440	08506	08561	08565	08587	08632	08652
08653	08682	08692	08710	08712	08733	08763	08770	08787	08793
08797	08798	08813	08839	08877	08900	08907	08910	08913	08921
08941	08942								
09007									

DRTC: **Departmental, Derby, Railway Technical Centre**

08814			
97204			
07403	97404		
97472	97480	97545	97561

DXXD: **Departmental, for reallocation**

08530	08576	08584	08767	08932

FABT (ex-FAMT): **Railfreight, Construction (Stone), Tinsley**

37380									
37411									
37676	37677	37678	37679	37680	37681	37682	37683	37684	37685
37686	37687	37688							

FACM (ex-FAMM): **Railfreight, Construction, Stone, Motherwell**

37370	37373	37379

FAGS (ex-FALG): **Railfreight, Construction, Stratford**

31116	31128	31134	31189	31198	31209	31234	31240	31293	31294
31296	31301	31306	31308	31320	31327				
37138	37144	37211	37218	37219					
37354									
47114	47229								
47325	47328	47367							

FAMA: **Railfreight, Construction (Stone), Thornaby**

31184	31215	31229

FAME: **Railfreight, Constuction (Stone), Eastfield**

47004	47006	47017	47210

FASB (ex-FALS): **Railfreight, Construction (Stone), Stewarts Lane**

33008	33009	33011	33012	33016	33020	33021	33022	33027	33029
33031	33033	33040	33042	33046	33047	33048	33050	33051	33052
33053	33055	33056	33057	33060	33063	33064			
33202	33204	33208	33211						

FAWK (ex-FAWC): **Railfreight, Construction (Stone), Cardiff**

37345									
37422	37425								
47033	47063	47079							
47320									
47901									
56001	56031	56032	56033	56034	56035	56036	56037	56038	56039
56040	56041	56043	56044	56045	56046	56048	56049	56050	56051
56052	56053	56055	56056	56057	56072				

Locomotive Sectors

FAXN (ex-FALX): Railfreight, Construction (Stone), Leicester

56042	56058	56059	56060	56061	56062	56063	56064	56065	56070
56078									

FAZZ: Railfreight, Construction, Shunters

08521	08532	08542	08544	08581	08593	08917	08923
09018							

FCCC (ex-FTLC): Railfreight, Chemicals, Crewe

31138									
47050	47186	47227	47228	47229					
47322	47323	47365							
47423	47425	47439	47440	47441	47442	47445	47446	47447	47449
47454	47456	47485	47491	47531	47532	47605			

FCTY (ex-FTYT): Railfreight, Chemicals, Thornaby

20008	20118	20119	20122	20137	20144	20156	20165
47301	47302	47303	47304	47305	47361	47362	47363

FEAK (ex-FECA): Railfreight, Coal, Trainload, Aberthaw, Cardiff

37701	37702	37703	37704	37796	37797	37798	37799	37800	37301
37802	37803	37887	37889	37894	37895	37896	37897	37898	37899

FEAN (ex-FENA): Railfreight, Coal, West Midlands

58001	58004	58005	58006	58007	58009	58010	58011	58012	
58013	58014	58015							

FEBN (ex-FENC): Railfreight, Coal, East Midlands

58002	58008	58016	58017	58018	58019	58020	58021	58022	58023
58024	58025	58026	58027	58028	58029	58030	58031	58032	58033
58034	58035	58036	58037	58038	58039	58040	58041	58042	58043
58044	58045	58046	58047	58048	58049	58050			

FECN (ex-FENB): Railfreight, Coal, Midlands

56002	56003	56004	56005	56006	56007	56008	56009	56010	56011
56012	56013	56014	56015	56016	56017	56018	56019	56020	56021
56022	56023	56024	56025	56026	56027	56028			

FEDN (ex-FEYA): Railfreight, Coal, Yorkshire, Toton

56029	56030	56047	56054	56066	56067	56068	56069	56071	56072
56073	56074	56075	56076	56077	56079	56080	56081	56082	56083
56084	56085	56086	56087	56088	56089	56090	56091	56092	56093
59094	56095	56096	56097	56098	56099	56100	56101	56102	56103
56104	56105	56106	56107	56108	56109	56110	56123		

FEEN (ex-FEYB): Railfreight, Coal, Trainload, Blythe

56111	56112	56113	56114	56115	56116	56117	56118	56119	56120
56121	56122	56124	56125	56126	56127	56128	56129	56130	56131
56132	56133	56134	56135						

FEFN (ex-FEND): Railfreight, Coal, East Midlands, Toton

20026	20047	20059	20071	20081	20084	20085	20094	20103	20104
20105	20108	20129	20131	20133	20134	20136	20140	20142	20151
20154	20157	20163	20166	20170	20177	20182	20186	20190	20194
20196	20210	20214	20215						

FEGN (ex-FENW): Railfreight, Coal, North-West, Toton

20004	20006	20007	20010	20013	20016	20019	20020	20021	20023
20040	20045	20051	20052	20053	20055	20057	20058	20065	20073
20075	20078	20080	20082	20087	20088	20090	20106	20113	20117
20120	20128	20130	20132	20135	20141	20143	20159	20168	20169
20175	20179	20187	20188	20197	20208				

FEOE (ex-FEGA): Railfreight, Coal, Scotland, Eastfield

20192	20198	20199	20205	20206	20211	20212	20213
37165	37229						
37375	37376						

FEPE (ex-FEGB): Railfreight, Coal, Lothians, Haymarket

26001	26002	26003	26004	26005	26006	26007	26008

FEZZ: Railfreight, Coal, Shunters, General

08434	08436	08610	08791	08893

FGWA: Railfreight, Distribution (Speedlink), Tinsley, Class 47

47002	47005	47012	47016	47049	47052	47060	47095	47097	47098
47102	47107	47110	47117	47120	47124	47142	47143	47144	47145
47146	47147	47150	47152	47156	47157	47188	47200	47201	47203
47204	47205	47206	47207	47209	47211	47213	47214	47215	47217
47218	47219	47220	47225	47226	47231	47234	47236	47237	47238
47241	47245	47249	47256	47258	47270	47279	47280	47283	47284
47285	47286	47287	47288	47289	47290	47292	47293	47296	47297
47298									
47306	47307	47308	47309	47310	47311	47312	47313	47314	47315
47316	47317	47321	47337	47338	47360	47370	47371	47372	47375
47376	47377	47378							
47421	47474	47588	47599	47600	47615				

FGWB: Railfreight, Distribution (Speedlink), Tinsley, Class 37

37003	37009	37013	37015	37029	37031	37058	37059	37062	37063
37065	37066	37071	37072	37073	37095	37096	37098	37101	37185
37194	37198	37242	37251	37270	37271	37285	37298		
37352	37353	37355	37356	37357	37378				

FGWC: Railfreight, Distribution (Speedlink), Tinsley, Class 31

31102	31108	31110	31113	31125	31126	31132	31142	31144	31145
31146	31147	31149	31155	31158	31159	31160	31163	31164	31166
31171	31174	31180	31248	31257	31259	31271	31284	31309	
31402	31466	31467							

FGWD: Railfreight, Distribution (Speedlink), Dover Link-span. Class 33/2. Stewarts Lane

33203	33205	33206

FGWE: Railfreight, Distribution (Speedlink), dc Electric, Stewarts Lane

73001	73002	73003	73004	73006
73106	73140	73141		

FGWS: Railfreight, Distribution (Speedlink), Eastfield

26025	26031	26032	26034	26037	26038	26040	26041

FGXX: Railfreight, Distribution (Speedlink), General

20009	20028	20035	20043	20069	20100	20145	20171	20172	20173
20185	20189	20218	20228					
37070	37109	37110	37114	37153	37196	37260		
37401	37402	37403	37404	37405	37406	37409	37410	37413	37423
37424								
47401	47402							

FGXZ: Railfreight, Speedlink, ac locomotives

81013	81017							
85004	85009	85010	85012	85015	85016	85018	85020	85021	85024
85026	85028	85031	85032	85035	85040			
90016	90017	90018						

FGZZ: Railfreight, Shunters, Distribution (Speedlink)

03170								
08388	08389	08397	08399	08405	08407	08410	08418	08419	08445
08447	08448	08454	08460	08466	08481	08489	08492	08495	08496
08498	08507	08510	08514	08516	08517	08519	08523	08526	08533
08539	08569	08570	08577	08580	08582	08589	08590	08591	08599
08620	08622	08627	08630	08631	08637	08649	08654	08656	08659
08661	08664	08672	08675	08690	08693	08695	08699	08700	08703
08705	08711	08713	08724	08725	08732	08737	08738	08739	08750
08754	08755	08778	08780	08781	08786	08792	08795	08799	08800
08802	08803	08819	08825	08826	08827	08832	08834	08838	08849
08853	08856	08881	08882	08887	08904	08905	08911	08912	08935
08937	08938	08939	08947	08948	08953	08956	08958		
09001	09010	09015	09022	09024	09025			

FHAC (ex-FHHA): Railfreight, (Coal), Flask, Crewe

31120	31130	31200	31217	31270	31275	31276	31312	31324

FHBK (ex-FHCC): Railfreight, Coal, Train-load, Cardiff

37689	37690	37691	37692	37693	37694	37695	37696	37697	37698
37699								

FHZZ: Railfreight, Shunters, Coal

08202	08308	08309	08375	08390	08402	08421	08428	08434	08436
08441	08442	08493	08508	08512	08535	08543	08586	08613	08623
08660	08686	08727	08729	08735	08769	08776	08782	08785	08796
08809	08818	08824	08870	08903	08946				
08993	08994	08995							

FJLL (ex-FTLL): Railfreight, Chemicals (China Clay) Laira. 071088

37421						
37669	37670	37671	37672	37673	37674	37575

FMCA: Railfreight, Metals (Steel), Cardiff

37197	37254	37278	37293
47281			
47359			

FMCC: Railfreight, Metals (Steel), Cardiff

37901	37902	37903	37904	37905	37906

FMCH: Railfreight, Metals (Steel), Cardiff

37710	37711	37712	37713	37714	37715	37716	37717	37718	37719
37883	37884	37885	37886						

FMGM: Railfreight, Metals, Ore, Hunterston

37010	37037	37040	37049	37051	37092	37137	37190	37201	37310
37311	37313	37320	37323	37324	37325	37326			

FMYI: Railfreight, Metals, Immingham

20025	20031	20044	20046	20061	20092	20093	20095	20098	20102
20107	20110	20112	20126						
37002	37042	37048	37054	37083	37106	37202	37203	37225	37241
37255	37258	37275							
37377	37381								

FMYT: Railfreight, Metals, Thornaby

37046	37069	37227	37240	37250					
37501	37502	37503	37504	37505	37506	37507	37508	37509	37510
37511	37512	37513	37514	37515	37516	37517	37518	37519	37520
37521	37667	37668							
47347									
47594									

FMXX: Railfreight, Metals, General

81004	81009					
86415	86418	86422	86423	86427	86432	86433

Locomotive Sectors

FMZZ: Railfreight, Shunters, Metals

08401	08485	08500	08509	08525	08537	08543	08594	08595	08603
08604	08615	08662	08665	08691	08694	08714	08749	08759	08920
08952	09008	09013							

FPGE: Railfreight, Petroleum and Chemicals, Eastfield

37035	37080	37113	37118	37188	37191	37232	37245
37359							

FPLC: Railfreight, Petroleum (Oil), Stanlow

47010	47085	47119	47125	47190	47193	47194	47195	47196	47233
47278									
47324	47368								

FPLI: Railfreight, Oil, Chemical, Construction, Immingham

31154	31156	31170	31185	31188	31199	31201	31203	31207	31210
31212	31221	31223	31225	31233	31238	31243	31249	31273	31284
31299	31302	31304	31319	31322					
47054	47115	47212	47221	47222	47223	47224	47276	47294	47295
47299									
47319	47336	47373	47374	47379	47380				
47411									

FPLW: Railfreight, Petroleum, South Wales

37078	37215	37221	37248	37280	37294	37306
37350	37371					
47094	47197	47198	47227			
47318	47326	47327	47369	47381		

FPLX: Railfreight, Petroleum, North Thames

31124	31152	31168	31311						
37705	37706	37707	37708	37709	37888	37890	37891	37892	37893

FPZZ: Railfreight, Petroleum, Shunters

08482	08734	08788	08877	08916

FQCK (ex-FQLC): Railfreight, Distribution (Speedlink), Coal, Cardiff

37131	37139	37162	37167	37212	37213	37214	37217	37222	37223
37230	37235	37239	37244	37294	37308				

FQZZ: Railfreight, Distribution (Speedlink), Coal, Shunters

08416	08829

FTZZ: Railfreight, Chemicals, Shunters

03162									
08423	08449	08463	08511	08575	08588	08663	08740	08743	08745
08751									

FVXX: Railfreight, Automotive, General

86413	86414
87101	

FVZZ: Railfreight, Shunters, Automotive

08601	08685	08688	08709	08758	08869	08873	08884	08902	08928

FXXA: Railfreight, General, for identification

08515	08747	08771	08886
33019	33035	33039	

FXXL: Railfreight, Shunters, General

08479	08532	08608	08646	08650	08668	08671	08756	08760	08779
08801	08804	08835	08837	08848	08850	08895	08896	08940	08945
08954	85006	85013	85036						

FXXS: Railfreight, General, Stored

IANA: InterCity, Anglia Region, Willesden

86214	86215	86216	86218	86220	86221	86223	86227	86229	86230
86232	86235	86237	86238	86244	86259	86260			

IANB: InterCity, Anglia, Shunters

08658	08752	08868

ICCA: InterCity, Cross-Country

08568	08571	08641	08644	08673	08854				
09020									
47470	47478	47512	47519	47520	47521	47525	47527	47551	47552
47556	47571	47577	47586	47589	47591	47593	47602	47606	47607
47608	47610	47612	47622	47629	47633	47636	47650	47651	47652
47653	47654	47655	47656	47657	47658	47659	47660	47664	47665
86206	86207	86210	86247	86248	86250	86253	86255		
86412	86439								
87009	87010	87031	87032						

ICHA: InterCity Charter

08556	08929								
45106									
47500	47508	47509	47555	47609	47620	47661	47662	47663	
86204	86856								
97251	97252								

Locomotive Sectors

IECA: **InterCity East Coast route**

08741	08874	08888	08957						
47471	47577								
89001									
91001	91002	91003	91004	91005	91006	91007	91008	91009	91010

IMAL: **InterCity Midland Region**

08536
47586

IVGA: **InterCity, Victoria-Gatwick**

09012									
73201	73202	73203	73204	73205	73206	73207	73208	73209	73210
73211	73212								

IWCA: **InterCity West Coast route**

08451	08609	08635	08648	08677	08680	08683	08717	08718	08765
08768	08808	08841	08846	08858	08901	08926	08934		
47459	47483	47517	47530	47544	47553	47562	47570	47578	47595
47597	47614	47618	47619	47629	47632	47637	47638	47639	47645
47646	47647	47648	47649						
81002	81005	81011							
83009	83012								
85005	85008	85030	85037	85038					
86101	86102	86103							
86208	86209	86224	86226	86236	86251	86252			
86405	86410	86419	86428	86430	86431	86437			
87001	87002	87003	87004	87007	87008	87011	87012	87014	87015
87016	87017	87018	87019	87020	87021	87022	87023	87024	87025
87026	87027	87028	87029	87030	87033	87034	87035		
90001	90002	90003	90004	90005	90006	90007	90008	90009	90010
90011	90012	90013	90014	90015	90020	90021	90022	90024	

IWCB: **InterCity West Coast route, TDM trials + BSO. Willesden**

86212	86219	86228	86231	86240	86241
86425				

IWRA: **InterCity Western Region**

08480	08483	08643	08645	08651	08949
47560	47590	47611	47613	47621	

LNRA: **Railfreight, Distribution (Freightliner), Class 37, Stratford**

37004	37012	37019	37038	37047	37053	37055	37057	37074	37075
37077	37087	37100	37104	37107	37116	37128	37154	37178	37209
37238	37252								
37358									

LNRB: **Railfreight, Distribution (Freightliner), Class 47, Stratford**

47007	47014	47096	47099	47100	47105	47108	47112	47116	47121
47123	47291								
47430	47452	47462							

LNRC: **Railfreight, Distribution (Freightliner), Class 47, Crewe**

47008	47009	47019	47051	47101	47187				
47330	47335	47343	47349	47350	47351	47354	47355	47364	
47451	47457	47479	47481						

LNRE: **Railfreight, Distribution (Freightliner), ac locomotives, Willesden**

86501	86502	86503	86504	86505	86506	86507	86508	86509	86510

LNRS: **Railfreight, Distribution (Freightliner), Shunters**

08413	08414	08415	08472	08667	08669	08689	08708	08811	08820
08823	08936								

LXXA: **Railfreight, Distribution (Freightliner) General**

47189									
81007	81010	81012							
85007	85034								
86402	86403	86404	86406	86407	86408	86409	86411	86416	86417
86420	86421	86435	86438						
87005	87006	87013							
90027	90028	90029							

NNEA: **Network SouthEast, Northwest, Stratford**

47576	47579	47581

NSSA: **Network SouthEast, Solent and Sarum, Laira**

47473	47547	47587	47598						
50001	50002	50003	50017	50018	50019	50027	50028	50029	50041
50043	50044	50048							

NSSB: **Network SouthEast, Solen and Sarum, Stewarts Lane**

73005			
73104	73112	73130	73134

NWRA: **Network SouthEast, Western Region. Old Oak Common**

47573	47582	74583	47598						
50023	50024	50025	50026	50030	50031	50032	50033	50034	50035
50036	50037	50039	50040	50046	50050				

NXXA: Network SouthEast, General

03179								
08670	08696	08698	08715	08828	08830	08845	08914	08933
09006	09016	09023						
85003								
86249	86257	86261						
86401								
97800								

PCFA: Provincial, Cardiff

08848							
37407	37408	37426	37427	37428	37429	37430	37431

PCRA: Provincial, Settle & Carlisle, Immingham, Class 47/4

47406	47407	47413

PEDA: Provincial, Eastfield

47701	47702	47703	47704	47705	47706	47707	47708	47709	47710
47711	47712	47714	47715	47716	47717				

PISA: Provincial, Inverness

08753								
37412	37415	37416	37417	37418	37419	37420		
47460	47461	47469	47492	47541	47563	47630	47635	37640	47641
47642	47643	47644						

PTPA: Provincial, North Trans-Pennine. Crewe

47422	47424	47434	47443	47444	47448	47475	47488	47503

PXXA: Provincial, General

03073									
08567	08616	08720	08731	08745	08761	08762	08777	08790	08851
08872	08915	08924							

RCWE: Parcels, dc Electric, Stewarts Lane

73141

RXLA: Parcels, General, Shunters

08527	08534	08538	08562	08578	08579	08585	08597	08611	08614
08617	08625	08633	08634	08676	08697	08704	08719	08721	08723
08730	08742	08744	08746	08748	08766	08805	08807	08821	08822
08833	08836	08840	08842	08844	08855	08857	08865	08875	08879
08890	08897	08899	08909	08918	08930	08944	08950	08951	08955
09002									

RXLB: Parcels, General, Class 31

31400	31404	31408	31410	31418	31421	31425	31427	31428	31429
31438	31442	31443	31450						

RXLD: Parcels, General, Class 47

47433	47435	47455	47458	47465	47466	47468	47476	47477	47482
47489	47490	47501	47515	47522	47523	47524	47526	47528	47533
47534	47535	47536	47537	47538	47539	47542	47543	47549	47557
47558	47559	47564	47565	47566	47567	45768	47569	47472	47574
47575	47580	47584	47585	47592	47603	47616	47624	47625	47626
47627	47631	47634							

RXLW: Parcels, General, ac Electric locomotives

85002	85011	85014	85019	85022	85023	85025
86213	86225	86234	86242	86243	86245	86254
86425	86426					

RXXA: Parcels, General

85022
90019

INTERCITY 125 POWER CARS
COSTING CENTRES/POOLS/SUB-SECTORS

ICCP: Cross Country, BRHQ

43012	43016	43019	43035	43036	43037	43126	43163	43164	43165
43166	43171	43172	43173	43174	43175	43177	43178	43179	43181
43182	43183	43184	43185	43186					

IECP: East Coast main line. Neville Hill

43013§	43014§	43040	43041	43042	43043	43052	43053	43054	43056
43057	43058	43059	43062	43063	43067	43068	43069	43070	43071
43074	43075	43078	43079	43080	43081	43082	43083	43084§	43085
43086	43087	43088	43089	43090	43091	43092	43093	43094	43095
43096	43097	43098	43099	43100	43101	43102	43103	43104	43105
43106	43107	43110	43111	43112	43113	43114	43115	43116	43117
43118	43119	43120	43121	43122	43123§	43154	43155	43156	43157
43159	43160	43194	43195	43196	43197	43198			

IMPL: Midland main line. Neville Hill

43038	43019	43044	43045	43046	43047	43048	43049	43050	43051
43055	43060	43061	43064	43065§	43066	43072	43073	43076	43077
43108	43109	43152	43153	43158	43161	43162	43193		

IWRP: Western Region: Bristol Bath Road

43002	43003	43004	43005	43006	43007	43008	43009	43010	43011
43015	43017	43018	43020	43021	43022	43023	43024	43025	43026
43027	43028	43029	43030	43031	43032	43033	43034	43124	43125
43127	43128	43129	43130	43131	43132	43133	43134	43135	43136
43137	43138	43139	43140	43141	43142	43143	43144	43145	43146
43147	43148	43149	43150	43151	43167	43168	43169	43170	43176
43180	43187	43188	43189	43190	43191	43192			

(§ Modified for DVT duties)

Privately Owned Steam Locomotives on TOPS — Number Conversion Table

Hist No	Class	Origin	TOPS Loco No	Name		Hist No	Class	Origin	TOPS Loco No	Name
1638	16xx	GWR	98238			2005	K1	LNER	98605	
3440	City	GWR	98240	City of Truro		841	S15	SR	98641	
46443	2MT	LMS	98243			3442	K4	LNER	98642	The Great Marquess
1000	4P	LMS	98400			5690	6P5F	LMS	98690	Leander
43106	4MT	LMS	98406			5593	6P5F	LMS	98693	Kolhapur
4027	4F	MR	98427			5596	6P5F	LMS	98696	Bahamas
4555	45xx	GWR	98455			70000	7P6F	BR Std	98700	Britannia
75069	4MT	BR Std	98469			34101	WC	SR	98701	Hartland
5572	45xx	GWR	98472			53809	7F	SDJR	98709	
80079	4MT	BR Std	98479			6115	7P	LMS	98715	Scots Guardsman
80080	4MT	BR Std	98480			34027	WC	SR	98727	Taw Valley
3882	0-6-0ST		98482	Barbara		7029	Castle	GWR	98729	Clun Castle
4588	45xx	GWR	98488			850	LN	SR	98750	Lord Nelson
5000	5MT	LMS	98500			5051	Castle	GWR	98751	Drysllwyn Castle
5305	5MT	LMS	98505	'Alderman A. E. Draper'		4771	V2	LNER	98771	Green Arrow
5407	5MT	LMS	98507			5080	Castle	GWR	98780	Defiant
7812	Manor	GWR	98512	Erlestoke Manor		34092	WC	SR	98792	City of Wells
7819	Manor	GWR	98519	Hinton Manor		6000	King	GWR	98800	King George V
5025	5MT	LMS	98525			6201	8P	LMS	98801	Princess Elizabeth
925	V	SR	98526	Cheltenham		35005	MN	SR	98805	Canadian Pacific
73129	5MT	BR Std	98529			60009	A4	LNER	98809	Union of South Africa
4930	Hall	GWR	98530	Hagley Hall		3822	2884	GWR	98822	
44932	5MT	LMS	98532			35028	MN	SR	98828	Clan Line
6960	Hall	GWR	98560	Raveningham Hall		46229	8P	LMS	98829	Duchess of Hamilton
2765	6P5F	LMS	98565			532	A2	LNER	98832	Blue Peter
44767	5MT	LMS	98567	'George Stephenson'		8233	8F	LMS	98833	
44871	5MT		98571	'Sovereign'		48151	8F	LMS	98851	
777	N15	SR	98577	Sir Lamiel		2857	28xx	GWR	98857	
6998	Hall	GWR	98598	Burton Agnes Hall		4468	A4	LNER	98868	Mallard
						4472	A3	LNER	98872	Flying Scotsman
						4498	A4	LNER	98898	Sir Nigel Gresley
						92220	9F	BR Std	98920	Evening Star

Notes:

The third character of Class 98 locomotive numbers represents the vehicle sub class, and the power classification of the locomotive, '9' are the largest locomotives and '0' are the smallest.

The last two characters of the locomotive number relate to the last two characters of the historic number. (Except when a clash occurs within a particular power range.)

Locomotive names shown between apostrophes, eg: 'George Stephenson' are not the historic name of the locomotive but have been allocated since preservation and may be currently carried on the locomotive.

Additional Information

The following amendments, advised to 20 February, require to be made to this publication covering changes effected during our production period.

Class 03: **Dimensions:** Add: 03-OCV before 03-ODX:
Train brakes: add: except *Diagram 03-OCV:* Vacuum only.
Sectors: delete *Network SouthEast,* add *Departmental:* **DCSB:** DCE Southern.
Note: add No 03079 formerly officially No 97805.
Add entry: 03079 CV *DCSB* RY.

Class 08: **Sectors:** *Departmental:* add **DCAB:** DCE Anglia. **DCEB:** DCE Eastern. **DXXD:** General, to be allocated.
Change **DWCS** to **DMES.**
Provincial: Add: **PCFA:** General, Cardiff. **PISA:** General, Inverness. *Railfreight:* delete **FXXA** and **LNRS.**
Entries: *Amend* No 08182 to read 08168 and 08335 to read 08331.
Delete (Withdrawn): 08250/58, 08468, 08716, 08898.
Allocations (Depot): 08449-IM, 08534-CL, 08595-DR, 08653-OC, 08745-NL, 08748-CA, 08837-RG, 08838-DY, 08928-BS, 08929-OC, 08947-WN.

Class 09: **Sectors:** *Departmental:* add **DMES:** DMEE, Shunters.
Allocations (Depot): 09007-SL.

Class 20: **Sectors:** Add *Private owner:* **CHUB:** Hunslet-Barclay.
Departmental: Change **DWCQ:** to **DMEA:.**
Railfreight: Change **FEGA:** to **FEOE, FEND** to **FEFN, FENW** to **FEGN, FTYT** to **FCYT.** *Delete:* **FGXX, FMGA.** *Add:*
FEOE: Coal, Scotland. **FGTE:** Distribution, Eastfield. **FGXI:** Distribution, Immingham. **FGXN:** Distribution, Toton.
Delete (Withdrawn): 20146, 20203.
Allocations (Depot): 20028-TO, 20041-ZQ, 20043-TO, 20060-ZQ, 20069-TO, 20083-ZQ, 20101-ZQ, 20145-ED, 20172/79-TO, 20185-ED, 20208-TO, 20209/19/24/25-ZQ, 20228-ED.

Classes 26/0 and 26/1: Maximum operating speed: Amend to 60mph (originally 80mph).
Sectors: *Departmental:* Change **DWCQ** to **DMEA.**
Railfreight: Change: **FEGB** to **FEPE, FGWS** to **FGSE.**

Class 31/1: **Maximum operating speed:** Amend to 60mph.
Sectors: *Departmental: Change:* **DWCQ** to **DMEA.**
Railfreight: Change: **FALG** to **FAGS, FAMA** to **FALY, FGWC** to **FGOT, FHHA** to **FHAC, FPLI** to **FPCI, FTLC** to
FCCC. Add: FPFS: Petroleum, North Thames.
Delete (Withdrawn): 31141/43, 31226/27, 31311.
Allocations (Depot): 31106-CD, 31124-SF, 31135/38-CD, 31149-TI, 31152/68-SF, 31230/52/55-CD,
31257/71/84-TI, 31289-SF, 31290-CD, 31293/96-SF, 31301-SF, 31322-IM.

Class 31/4: **Sectors:** *Departmental:* Change: **DWCQ** to **DMEA.**
Railfreight: Change: **FGWC** to **FGOT.**
Provincial: Delete: **PXXA.**
Allocations: 31403-07/09/10/19/22/23/24/48/51/54/55/59/62/63/64-BS.

Class 33/0: **Maximum operating speed:** Amend to 60mph (originally 85mph).
Sectors: *Departmental: Add:* **DMEA:** DMEE General.
Railfreight: Change: **FALS** to **FASB.** *Delete:* **FPXX.**
Network SouthEast. Delete: **NSSB.**
Delete (Withdrawn): 33031.
Named: Add: 33025 *Sultan.*
Allocations (Depot): 33064-SL.

Late Information/Notes

Class 33/1: Add Maximum operating speed: 85mph.
Sectors: *Departmental: Add:* **DMEA:** DMEE General.
Network SouthEast: Delete: **NSSB.**
Named: *Delete:* 33114 *Sultan.*

Class 33/2: Sectors: *Railfreight: Change:* **FALS** to **FASB, FGWD** to **FGWB.**
Add (Reinstated): 33202   AX   Fa   *FASB*   SL
Delete (Withdrawn): 33209.

Class 37/0: Sectors: *Railfreight: Change:* **FEGA** to **FEOE, FGWB** to **FGET, FMCA** to **FMAK, FMYT** to **FMTY,**
FPGE to **FPAE, FPLW** to **FPEK, FQLC** to **FQCK.** *Add:* **FAGS:** Construction, Stratford. **FGDS:** (ex-LNRA)
Distribution, Stratford. **FGUV:** Distribution, Inverness. *Delete:* **FGXX, FMCH.**
Freightliner: Delete **LNRA** (Now FGDS).
Renumbering: Add: 37303 = 37271, 37304 = 37272, 37306 = 37273, 37308 = 37274, 37374 = 37165.
Add: (Reclassified and renumbered) 37165 KX   x   F   *FEOE*   ED.
Move data (Renumbered): 37303, 37271 to 37304 to 37272, 37306 to 37273, 37308 to 37274, 37312 to
37137, 37321 to 37037.
Named: 37275 *Stainless Pioneer.*
Allocations (Depot): 37227/40/50-TE.

Class 37/3: Sectors: *Railfreight: Change:* **FAMM** to **FACM, FAMT** to **FABT, FGWB** to **FGET,** Add: **FAWK**
Construction (Stone), Cardiff. **FEOE:** Coal, Scotland. **FGDS:** Distribution, Stratford. **FPAE:** Petroleum & Chemicals,
Eastfield. **FPLW:** Petroleum, Wales, Cardiff. *Delete:* **FPLX, FQLC.**
Delete (Reclassified): 37374.
Allocations (Depot): 37350/54-CF, 37375/76-ED.

Class 37/4: Sectors: *Departmental: Delete* **DCHA.**
Railfreight: Change: **FAWC** to **FAWK.** *Add:* **FABT:** Construction (Stone), Tinsley. **FGTE:** Distribution, Eastfield.
FGUV: Distribution, Inverness. **FJLL:** Chemicals (China Clay), Laira. *Delete:* **FGXX, FMGA.**
InterCity: Delete: **ICHA, IWCA.**
Provincial: Add: **PCFA:** General, Cardiff. *Delete:* **PXXA.**
Allocations (Depot): 37407/08-CF, 37411-TI, 37412-LA, 37422/25-CF.

Class 37/5: Sectors: *Railfreight: Change:* **FAMT** to **FABT, FHCC** to **FHBK, FMYT** to **FMTY, FTLL** to **FJLL.**

Class 37/7: Sectors: *Railfreight: Change:* **FECA** to **FEKK, FMCH** to **FMHK, FPLX** to **FPFS.**

Class 37/9: Sector: *Railfreight: Change:* **FMCC** to **FMCK.**

Class 43: Named: Add: 43108 *BBC Television Railwatch.* 43191 *Seahawk.*
43192 *City of Truro. Delete:* 43002/61/92/96/98, 43100/01/02/05/07/10/21/26/31/42/88.

Class 45/1: Delete: Special Livery.
Delete (Withdrawn): 45106.
Add (Reinstated): 45128 AX *ICHA* TI.

Class 47/0: Sectors: *Departmental: Delete:* **DCHA.**
Railfreight: Add: **FAGS:** Construction (Stone), Stratford. **FGBC** (ex-LNRC) Distribution, Crewe. **FGCS** (ex-LNRB)
Distribution, Stratford. *Change:* **FAWC** to **FAWK, FGWA** to **FGAT, FPLC** to **FPBC, FPLI** to **FPCI, FPLW** to **FPEK,**
FTLC to **FCCC.**
Freightliner: Delete: **LNRB** (now FGCS), **LNRC** (now FGBC).
Add (Reinstated): 47145   EX   *FGAT*   TI
                                  47189   EX   *FGBC*   CD (sDL)
Delete (Withdrawn): 47235.
Dia: *Change:* **LX:** 47054. **NX:** 47222/24/94.
Allocation (Depot): 47115-IM, 47124-TI, 47186/87-CD, 47229-SF, 47277-CF.

Class 47/3: Diagram: *Sectors: Railfreight: Add:* **FCTY:** Chemicals, Thornaby. **FGBC:** (ex-LNRC) Distribution, Crewe. *Change:* **FALG** to **FAGS, FAWC** to **FAWK, FGWA** to **FGAT, FMYT** to **FMTY, FPLI** to **FPCI, FPLW** to **FPEK, FTLC** to **FCCC.**
Freightliner: *Delete* **LNRC** (now FGBC).
Dia: *Change:* **BX:** 47319/36/73/74.
Allocations (Depot): 47320-CF.

Class 47/4: Sectors: *Departmental, Add:* **DCEA:** DCE, Eastern Region.
Railfreight: Add: **FGBC:** Distribution, Crewe. **FGCS:** Distribution, Stratford. **FGXI:** Distribution, Immingham. **FPCI:** Petroleum, Immingham. *Change:* **FGWA** to **FGAT, FMYT** to **FMTY, FTLC** to **FCCC.**
Provincial: *Add* **PISA:** General, Inverness. *Delete:* **PXXA.**
Allocations (Depot): 47481-CD, 47515-BR, 47542-ED, 47572/74-BR, 47578-ED, 47580/85-BR, 47596-OC, 47598-LA.

Class 47/7: Sector: *Provincial: Add:* **PEDA** *General, ScotRail Express, Eastfield. Delete:* **PXXA.**

Class 47/9: Sector: *Railfreight: Change:* **FAWC to FAWK.**

Class 50: Diagram: *Add* 50-OBX, Maximum operating speed 60mph.
Sectors: *Delete:* **RXXA.**
Delete (Withdrawn): 50012.
Dia. *Change:* **BX:** 50004/05/07/08/09/15/16/20/21/42/45.

Class 50/1: Maximum operating speed: *Change:* 60mph (originally 100mph as Class 50/0).
Sectors: Add *Departmental:* **DCWA:** DCE, Western Region.
Railfreight: Delete.

Class 56: Sectors: *Railfreight: Change:* **FALX** to **FAXN, FAWC** to **FAWK, FENB** to **FECN, FEYA** to **FEDN, FEYB** to **FEEN.**
Allocations (Depot): 56072-TO.

Class 58: Sectors: *Railfreight: Change:* **FENA** to **FEAN, FENC** to **FEBN.**
Named: *Add:* 58003 *Markham Colliery.*

Class 73/0: Sectors: *Add: Railfreight:* **FGWE:** Distribution, dc electric locomotives.

Class 73/1: Sectors: *Departmental:* **DMEA:** DMEE General. *Railfreight: Add:* **FGWE:** Distribution, dc electric locomotives. *Delete:* **FALS.**

Class 81: Delete (Withdrawn): 81005/06/19.

Class 85: Delete (Withdrawn): 85022.

Class 86/2: Delete (Reclassified and renumbered): 86239/41.

Class 86/5: Add data: 86507 (86239) BX s I *LNRE* WN *L. S. Lowry*
86508 (86241)† BX I *LNRE* WN *Glenfiddich*

Class 87/0: Renamed: 87006 *City of Glasgow.*

Class 89: Named: 89001 *Avocet.*

Class 90: Allocations: 90020-23 -ZQ.

Class 97/0: Delete (Reclassified): Diagram 97-0EV and 97805 (see Class 03).

Class 97/7: Sector: *Departmental: Add* **DMEX:** DMEE, Battery-electric locomotives. *Delete:* **DCEA, DCMA.**

Late Information/Notes

Special Purpose Locomotives. **Allocations (Depot):** ADB 968021 -ZQ.
InterCity 125 Coaching Stock.
Reclassified and renumbered: 40228 0A R I /WR PM. (ex- 40428). 40724 0A R I /WR LA (ex-40324). Delete
(Withdrawn): 42126, 44027.
Diagrams: *30E:* 42254/55/56/58/62/63/64/67/68/70/71/72/74/75/76/78/87/88/91/92/95/96/99, 42300
30F: 42341
30H: 42024/25/45/46, 42104/24/27/33/34/38/66-72/75/76/77/83-88/91/92/95-98, 42200-03/05-08/10-13/17/
18/22/23/25/26/27/37/38/41/42/46/47/48
30J: 42257/65/66/69/82/89/93/97, 42301
30K: 42023/26/47/78, 42103/05/06/07/22/28/32/73/74/82/89/90/93/99, 42204/09/14/19/24/28-31/39/49
30L: 42003/04/09/10/12/13/21/22
30M: 42005/11/14.
Allocations (Depot): 40741-HT, 40749-NL, 41111/12-NL, 41153/54-HT, 42195-NL, 42205/09-HT,
42227/28-NL, 44020-NL, 44070-HT, 44073-NL, 44083-HT, 44097-BN.
Formations: *Class 253* In second set headings after 'GK4' add 'GN4§'.
Unit 30: Change 40324 to 40724†.
Unit 36: Add R, change 40428 to 40228§.
Unit 50: Delete 42196, change 44020 to 44084. *Spare:* Delete 44084.
Class 254: Amend units to read:
28 R /ML NL 41112 41111 40741 -- 42195 42220 42227 42228 44073.
35 P /EC HT 41153 41154 40511* 41066* 40749* 42205 42210 -- 44083.
38 *Change:* 42126 and 44027 to read 42196 44020.

SPECIAL CHARACTERISTICS: The following additions are applicable:
B: 37430/31, 47007/08/12/16/18/19/49/50/52/54/60/95/97, 47102/07/20/20/24/44/56/57/88/93/94/97, 47203-06/
09/14/15/17/18/20/26/28/31/33/34/36/37/38/41/45/49/78/80/83/84/85/87-92/96/97/98, 47301/06-09/14/15/
19/20/21/36/37/44/47/53/55/58/60/70-73/76, 47406/11/13/17/21/22/25/26/31/32/33/40/43/50/51/52/56/57/
59/74/75/79/89/91, 47500/03/15/18/19/30/36/42/43/56/58/66/79/81/89/90/92, 47606/12/13/15/21/24/37/39/
47/52/55/56/58/60/62/63/64, 50015, 56004/05/12/14-17/19/27/30/33/37/42/51/54/57/59/61/63-99, 56100-11/
13-35, 58004/06/12/16/26/27/31/33/35/37/38/39/43/44/45/47/48/50.
C: 08567/71/83, 08624, 08770, 08800, 08903/06/08.
R: 37430/31.
U: 33211.
X: 47222/24/94, 47319/36/73/74.
60: 50004/05/07/08/09/15/16/20/21/42/45.
The following deletions are advised:
B: 86225.
K: 20118/19/22, 37196.
75: 47596, 47607.
InterCity 125 Coaching Stock:
R: 41021/22, 41137/38, 42030/31/32, 42283/84/85, 44010/36.
-: 42030/31/32, 42283/84/85.

SECTORS: The following have changed Sector/sub-Sector ownership. Where the sub-Sector code only has been
changed (as indicated above) a full listing of locomotives involved appears on preceding pages.
CHUB: 20041/60/83, 20101, 20209/19/24/25.
DCAB: 08528/29/31/40/41, 08638, 08757/72/75, 08810/59/89. *DCEB:* 08499, 08583, 08605/07/18/55/57,
08701/06/73/83/94, 08866/67/70/76/85, 08906/08/19/31. *DCMA:* 20056, 20121/78, 31403-07/09/10/19/22/23/
24/48/51/54/55/59/62/63/64. *DCMB:* 08624. *DCSA:* 33058, 73107/11/38/39. *DCSB:* 03179. *DCWA:* 47334/41,
50149.
DMEA: 20202, 31289, 31460, 33025, 33111, 73136. *DMES:* 08632/52, 08734/87, 09007. *DMEX:* 97701-08.
DXXD: 08530/76/84, 08767, 08932.

FABT: 37411. *FAGS:* 31189, 31293/96, 31301/20, 47325. *FASB:* 33046/48/52/63/64, 33204. *FAWK:* 37354, 37422/25, 47320. *FAZZ:* 08521/42/44/93, 08923. *FCCC:* 31138, 47186. *FCTY:* 47301-05/61/62/63.
FEAN: 58017. *FEDN:* 56072. *FEGN:* 20088, 20187, 20208. *FEOE:* 37165, 37375/76.
FGAT: 47124. *FGBC:* 47187, 47451/57/79/81. *FGCS:* 47430/52/62. *FGDS:* 37358. *FGOT:* 31149, 31257/71/84.
FGTE: 20145/85, 20228, 37401-06/09/10/13/23/24. *FGUV:* 37070, 37109/10/14/53/96, 37260, 37412/14-20.
FGWE: 73001-04/06, 73106/40/41. *FGXI:* 20009/35, 20171, 47401/02. *FGXN:* 20028/43/69, 20100/72/73/89,
20218. *FGXZ:* 90016/17/18. *FGZZ:* 08413/14/15/72, 08516/39/77, 08659/69/89, 08708/60, 08811/17/20/23/38/
78, 08936/47.
FHZZ: 08308/09, 08434/36, 08586, 08880.
FJLL: 37421. *FMTY:* 37227/40/50. *FMZZ:* 08401, 08500/09/25/37/94/95, 08662/65/91, 08714/49.
FPAE: 37359. *FPCI:* 31170, 31221, 31322, 47115, 47221/94, 47411. *FPFS:* 31124/52/68. *FPLW:* 37215/94,
37350, 47277. *FPZZ:* 08871.
FQZZ: 08806.
FTZZ: 08575/88, 08740/43/51.
FVZZ: 08709/58, 08869/73, 08928.
FXXL: 08515, 08837/87.
ICHA: 08929. *IECP:* 43065. *IMLP:* 43043. *IWCA:* 47578. *IWCB:* 86425.
NSSB: 73130/34. *NWRA:* 47596. *NXXA:* 08670, 08715, 08828.
PCFA: 08848, 37407/08/26-31. *PEDA:* 47701-12/14-17. *PISA:* 08753, 47460/61/69/92, 47541/63,
47630/35/40-44. *PXXA:* 08567, 08745, 08872.
RXLA: 08719/66, 08833. *RXLC:* 33101/02/03/06/14. *RXLE:* 86424. *RXXA:* 90019.

InterCity 125 Coaching Stock:
IEC: 40741, 41153/54, 42205/10, 44083, 44100.
IML: 40749, 41111/12, 42196, 42227/28, 44020/73.

LIVERIES: The following revised liveries have been reported:
Departmental: **D:** 31412/52/53.
InterCity: **I:** 43006/08/29/50/73/76/80/91/94, 43106/07/08/10/17/21/29/30/39/42/61/64/65/88/91/92, 47470,
47520/66/70/90, 47619/25, 73104/14/38/40, 90020-23.
Network SouthEast **N:** 03179, 47596/98.
Provincial **Pt:** 47475.
Railfreight: **F-:** 08506, 26008, 37902/03/04/06, 47335/54/65, 47605/15.
Fa: 08542, 08923, 33033/42/63, 33204, 47063, 47114, 56032/50/62.
Fe: 08512, 08791, 26001/07, 31120/30, 31200/17/70/75/76, 31312/24, 37167, 37235/74, 56003/12-15/29/47/
69/72/80/84/88/90/92/94/95, 56104/27/28/29, 58006/09/11/12/16/25.
Fg: 08407/60, 08737, 37047/63, 37101/94/98, 37271/72, 37355/56/57, 47052, 47117/50/56/87,
47201/14/41/58.
Fm: 08665, 08920, 37037/49, 37106/37, 37201/02/75/78, 47347.
Fp: 31201/73, 37080, 37215, 47010/54/94, 47336/68.

InterCity 125 Coaching Stock: *InterCity:* **I:** 41021/22, 41137/38, 42030/31/32, 42283/84/85, 44010/36/97/98.

LOCOMOTIVE COSTING CENTRES
Stop Press
Changed codes: FAMA now FALY, FGWA now FGAT, FGWB now FGET, FGWC now FGOT, FGWD now FGWB,
FGWS now FGSE, FGXX divided to FGUV, FGTE, FGXI, FGXN; FMCA now FMAK, FMCC now FMCK, FMCH now
FMHK, FMTY now FMYT, FPGE now FPAE, FPLC now FPBC, FPLI now FPCI, FPLW now FPEK, FPLX now FPFS,
LNRA now FGSE, LNRB now FGCS, LNRC now FGBC, LNRS deleted, added to FGZZ.
New codes: **.DMEX:** Departmental, DMEE, Battery-electric locomotives; **FGTE:** Distribution, Eastfield; **FGUV:**
Distribution, Inverness; **FGXI:** Distribution, Immingham; **FGXN:** Distribution, Toton.

DMEX: 97701-08. (Delete from DCEA or DMEA)
FALS: delete 33031.

Late Information/Notes

FGTE: 20145/85, 20228, 37401-06/09/23/24.
FGUV: 37070, 37109/10/14/53/96, 37260, 37414-21.
FGXI: 20009/35, 20171, 47401/02.
FGXN: 20028/43/69, 20100/72/73/89, 20218.
FJLL: Delete 37421, Add 37412.
FPLX: Delete 31311.
FXXA to *FXXL:* 08515, 08747/71, 08886.
ICHA: Delete 45106, Add 45128.
IWCA: Delete 81005.
PISA: Delete 37412/15-20.
RXXA: Delete 85022.

43111
43154
31293
31204

37019
38072
        37085
        37068